ENERGY
for Life

About the Author

Colleen Deatsman has been exploring personal spiritual development and healing, and incorporating these learnings into therapy and workshop trainings, for over twenty-five years. She is a Licensed Professional Counselor, Registered Social Worker, Reiki Master, Certified Hypnotherapist, Certified Alternative Healing Consultant, Shamanic Practitioner, and owner and sole practitioner of the private practice Circle of Life Counseling Services. She is a frequent contributor to several local and statewide publications on spiritual enlightenment, health and wellness, and self-healing.

To Write to the Author

If you wish to contact the author or would like more information about this book, please write to the author in care of Llewellyn Worldwide and we will forward your request. Both the author and publisher appreciate hearing from you and learning of your enjoyment of this book and how it has helped you. Llewellyn Worldwide cannot guarantee that every letter written to the author can be answered, but all will be forwarded. Please write to:

Colleen Deatsman
⁒ Llewellyn Worldwide
2143 Wooddale Drive, Dept. 0-7387-0774-0
Woodbury, Minnesota 55125-2989, U.S.A.
Please enclose a self-addressed stamped envelope for reply,
or $1.00 to cover costs. If outside of the U.S.A.,
enclose international postal reply coupon.

Many of Llewellyn's authors have websites with additional information and resources. For more information, please visit our website at www.llewellyn.com.

COLLEEN DEATSMAN

ENERGY
for Life

CONNECT WITH THE SOURCE

Llewellyn Publications
Woodbury, Minnesota

First Edition
First Printing, 2006

Book design by Steffani Chambers
Cover art © 2006 by Digital Vision
Cover design by Ellen Dahl
Edited by Karin Simoneau
Llewellyn is a registered trademark of Llewellyn Worldwide, Ltd.

Library of Congress Cataloging-in-Publication Data
Deatsman, Colleen, 1960–
    Energy for life: connect with the source / Colleen Deatsman.—1st ed.
      p. cm.
    Includes bibliographical references.
    ISBN-13: 978-0-7387-0774-7
    ISBN-10: 0-7387-0774-0
      1. Energy—Therapeutic use. 2. Vital force—Therapeutic use. 3. Mental healing.
    4. Self-care, Health. I. Title.

RZ421.D42 2006
615.8'51—dc22   2006040982

Llewellyn Worldwide does not participate in, endorse, or have any authority or responsibility concerning private business transactions between our authors and the public.

All mail addressed to the author is forwarded but the publisher cannot, unless specifically instructed by the author, give out an address or phone number.

Any Internet references contained in this work are current at publication time, but the publisher cannot guarantee that a specific location will continue to be maintained. Please refer to the publisher's website for links to authors' websites and other sources.

Note: The techniques presented in *Energy for Life* are not intended to replace medical or psychological treatment.

Llewellyn Publications
A Division of Llewellyn Worldwide, Ltd.
2143 Wooddale Drive, Dept. 0-7387-0774-0
Woodbury, Minnesota 55125-2989, U.S.A.
www.llewellyn.com

Printed in the United States of America

Other Books by Colleen Deatsman

Inner Power: Six Techniques for Increased Energy & Self-Healing

For Pat and Lauren
I love you!

Special Thanks:

Paul Bowersox, writing and editorial wizard. I thank you from the bottom of my heart and soul for your writing and editorial contributions, brilliance, in-depth guidance and teachings, energy concept explanations, time, energy, resources, expertise, insights, bluntness, constructive criticism, tear-wiping, compassion, understanding, support, and for sharing the solitude of the swamp. This book would not be what it is without you!

My Beloved Family: Pat, Lauren, Laura, Erin, Mom and Dad Deatsman, Mom Kelley, Greg, Kris, Maureen, Rick, and Kolleen for supporting my dreams.

The Helping Spirits who orchestrated and guided this journey.

The phenomenal friends, Spirit workers, and healers that I am blessed to sit in circle with who have supported the birth of my books and my growth with their unconditional love and personal teachings: Michael, Durrette, Carlton, Fawn, Pat, Jan, Brenda, Marisa, Terri, Jason, Tammy, Rochele, Barb, Clint, Angie, Tammy, Brenda, Steve, Betsy, Miriam, Jen, Kate, Eryn, Signe, Diana, John, Carol, Arlene, Joy, Laurie, and Karen.

Judy, my dearly beloved wisewoman mentor, colleague, and soul-comrade.

Stephanie Clement, acquisitions editor, Llewellyn Publications, whose vision made this book a reality.

Carrie Obry, Next Step acquisitions editor, and Karin Simoneau, new titles editor, Llewellyn Publications, for your insightful editorial suggestions and corrections.

Llewellyn Publications, for opening minds, hearts, and souls around the world.

CONTENTS

Activities

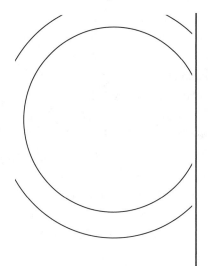

ENERGIZE
YOURSELF!

Introduction

The golden rays of the new morning sun peek out from behind the mountaintops, lending a ghostly orange glow to the thick fog on the lake. The dawn mist feels damp and chilly, but this promise of a sunny day sends whispers of warmth throughout the wilderness. The crow caws from the top bough of the mighty virgin pine as the diffuse sunbeams accentuate his black silhouette. As if signaled by the impending sunrise, the loon, who has been fishing quietly next to my canoe, extends his neck and sends his eerie call out into the solitude. Shivers run down my spine and my heart aches with a deep soul connection with this beautiful being. His call travels over the lake and up the mountains, circling around and echoing back down. As the sunbeams lengthen across the lake, the mighty pines change from their nightly black dress into their daytime green, and a gentle breeze rustles the boughs. Stretching higher into the clear blue sky, the sun ascends the mountain summit and makes his full, grand entrance into the day. The brilliance of his power blinds my eyes and I reluctantly turn away. As I do, I catch the movement of a large bird soaring through the dissipating yellow fog.

A moment later, the mysterious bird sends her eerie call out into the wild and is easily identified as another loon. Her mate, sitting near me, returns her call and instantly she splashes down next to us. As the ripples of the clear spring-fed lake calm, she rises up on her feet and appears to be dancing as she fluffs and dries her wings. The two talk back and forth to each other in a laughing, chattering dialect, and I am thrilled to bear witness to their interplay. Settling in next to her fishing partner, she too begins to search the crystal waters for her shiny breakfast. As the morning grows deeper into day, the breeze strengthens and sighs through the dense forest surrounding the lake. Soaring high above the mountaintop, the hawk cries, drawing my attention upward to watch her embrace the new day. A low grunting sound moves up the river behind me, toward the lake. The source exposes itself as a huge, great blue heron soars in, extends its landing gear, and comes to rest on the beaver lodge. The beaver, who is gathering leafy twigs on the other side of the small lake, doesn't seem to mind the visitor and continues to go about his work.

A powerful supernatural energy moves in my body as I sit melted in divine connection with these vibrant beings and this pristine wilderness. My body and soul fill with reverent wonder. I feel whole, peaceful, healthy, and vital here in the quiet solitude of the wilderness, where the song of the universe sings deep in my soul. Surrounded by this incredible life-force, my heart fills with gratitude and I thank the Spirits and the creator for blessing me. By allowing myself to sit quietly and "just be," I have given myself a gift of energy beyond measure.

A few moments later, my voice on the self-recorded guided journey tape indicates that it is time to return to my ordinary activities. In my soft space in my home, I come back into my body. I am reluctant to leave this inspiring place of power, but I am thankful to have learned methods that allow me to visit as often as I want.

Upon returning from my guided journey, I take a few minutes to write my thoughts and feelings in my journal, feel my body, and integrate my experience. Powerful universal life-force energy and a deep sense of well-being flow through me.

For many summers, I have been going to this lake in northern Canada to replenish my energy in the solitude of the wilderness, and I have been blessed with many experiences such as this. When I am there, I am free and wild like the wilderness that surrounds me. Universal energy flows through me, healing my body from the ravages of the everyday world. If I could live in this place, I would always be a direct recipient of this empowering energy. However, like most everyone, I am not able to live in an awesome place of solitude that feeds my soul. I live in a wonderful place, but it is in a world of busyness and responsibility, where the daily barrage can result in tension, high stress, energy loss, and fatigue. If I were unable to or didn't know how to replenish my energy and repair the effects of stress, this energy loss would multiply into chronic fatigue and a host of mysterious syndromes that elude medical cure.

I learned this the hard way—by experience. In a desperate search for healing during my ten-year struggle with chronic fatigue immune deficiency syndrome, fibromyalgia, asthma, and environmental illness, I became an expert on how to energize and heal myself. I discovered that journeying, meditating, and utilizing energy connecting exercises link me to the same energizing power that replenishes my energy while in solitude—and this can be accessed no matter where I am. Just a few minutes of conscious intention unites me with powerful energy that I then bring into my everyday activities to keep my soul connected, my emotions calm, my thoughts clear, and my body energized. You can easily do the same. The activities taught in this book, along with the accompanying CD, will show you how to make this happen.

· · ·

Energy for Life is the book and CD combination that will change the way you think about and utilize energy. It is full of potent energy connecting ideas and exercises that you will use for years to come. It is a powerful resource that you will refer to often for ways to reclaim your natural link to the dynamic energy in yourself and the universe. *Energy for Life* will help you cope in our stress-filled world. You will recommend it to others because it is helpful, but when asked to borrow it, you might be reluctant to let it go.

Energy for Life opens the doors of understanding and teaches you the practical skills you need to manifest powerful energy in your everyday life. Through succinct explanations, step-by-step instructions, and revitalizing activities, you will learn about energy, activate your own personal life-force energy, release blockages, stop energy leakages, and power up through direct connection with universal life-force, spiritual, and source energies. Functional ideas for easily applying and integrating the activities in your daily life are included to help you manifest vitality.

Feeling vibrant and full of abundant energy is our perfect state of being. After all, we and our world are made of energy, an essence and a force that is full of potent power. All of the wisdom teachings and great faiths of the world make mention of this force that surrounds and moves through all of us. It is often described as healing and enlightening, and as a creative essence that can be marshaled to guide lives and make miracles happen. This force is commonly known to modern-day researchers and energy workers as *life-force energy*. Of course, there are innumerable ways to refer to the stratum, layers, and shadings that compose the limitless energies in the universe.

To simplify a vast and complicated subject, I have chosen six terms to sum up energy throughout the book.

- *Proto-singularity*, or *the singularity*, refers to the unformed, unmanifest, pregnant void from which all potential emanates. The singularity is the mother of the gods. Before matter, before thought, before the thinnest manifestation of the most ethereal plane, there is the singularity of potential.

- *Universal life-force energy* is the first emanation that comes from this potential. It is the formless, pervasive, causal undercurrent of all that is. Universal life-force energy is the divine intelligence, the engine of creation, the cosmic grid upon which and from which the universe springs.

- Universal life-force energy densifies and differentiates, driving its own energy to coalesce into the fundamental energies of the manifest universe. I will refer to the undifferentiated universal life-force energy that has yet to be "directed" or apportioned as *source energy*.

- Over time, the energies become denser until the physical universe comes into being. The shadings progress through the subtler spirit energies, eventually producing all forms of both subtle and gross matter. These forms are part of the spirit and material worlds and are imbued with their own radiant energy, a by-product of being made up of high-powered universal life-force energy. This radiant energy is *life-force energy*. It can be thought of as the emanation of Gaia, and includes all the natural and various spiritual energies. life-force energy is the observable energy inherent in the manifest universe. It is energy associated with form.

- Finally, we call the innate and unique energy of our being our *personal life-force energy*.

To further clarify, everything, everywhere can be viewed as being made from universal life-force energy. All other energies we can define fall somewhere on the spectrum of varying densities of universal life-force energy. Gross matter in the material world is universal life-force energy at its most dense. A bit lighter is life-force energy, an emanation of the world of form. Associated with life-force energy are the spiritual energies. These are energies associated with form, just not physical form. Angels, spirit guides, all our deities, and ascended masters are spirit energies. What we have chosen to call universal life-force energy itself, is the energy that permeates everything, the formless platform upon which all else exists. In many ways, the terms "life-force energy", "spiritual energy", and "universal life-force energy" are interchangeable. All represent the subtle energies inherent in the world of form, but while life-force energy is the energy associated with form itself, and spiritual energy is that life-force energy associated with the lighter spirit realms alone, universal life-force energy remains the unseen backdrop of all that is, formed, unformed, and spirit. The least dense on the spectrum is source energy. It is universal life-force energy at its purest, lightest essence, the first emanation of the singularity of potential. Formless, non-dual, ultra high-powered and clear, it is pure divine intelligence as yet undirected. Before this, and entirely out of our reach, is the proto-singularity, the progenitor of the manifest."

We'll progressively expand on these terms and concepts throughout the course of this book

We begin in chapter 1, where we learn about the basics of energy—what it is, what modern science knows of it, what the ancients knew about it, and how they accessed it for healing, guidance, and survival. I'll explain why and how connecting with revitalizing energy is instrumental to our quality of life and continued survival. I'll introduce basic skills that will help you begin to access this source of power, and we'll further expand on them to deepen your connection throughout the book and your practice.

This life-force energy permeates all of us—it runs through us as the vital energy that gives us life. The energy that is uniquely ours, our personal life-force energy, is the focus of chapter 2. What it is, how it works, and why we need to stimulate and circulate it for revitalization is the focus of key activities that initiate controlled access to your internal power.

Most of us in the West don't need to worry about where our next meal is coming from or if we will end up on some other creature's menu. We stay safe and warm, cradled in the arms of technology, behind the walls of our comfortable homes. We have been able to turn away from the dire needs of survival, but in doing so have also turned away from the natural sources of life and forgotten the primal energies at our disposal.

However, the truth is that we all have a beautiful energy field and a natural ability to connect with all of the energies around us, as we read in chapters two, three, and four. We know this as children, but soon forget how to stay connected with energy as we get caught up in daily life. The pressures of societal conditioning, academic learning, fitting into society, making a living, raising children, and so on capture our attention, and we focus on the external aspects of making our lives happen. We are taught myriad different skills, like how to balance a checkbook or how to increase our productivity, but we have not been taught about energy, or how and why it would be beneficial for us to access it. Bombarded with constant stress, busyness, and a lack of basic energetic self-care, patterns and behaviors that unconsciously develop over time dangerously drain our personal life-force energy. The blockage and leakage busting activities in chapters 3 and 4 address the challenges born out of this shift away from our once natural connection with life-force energy.

Once you have a mental concept of energy, reconnect with your personal life-force energy, and clear away your blockages and leakages, it's time to access the powerhouse of health and vitality—life-force energy and universal life-force energy. Chapter 5 will equip you with the skills necessary to invite universal life-force energy into your body, mind, emotions, energy field, soul, and life. This is accomplished through a simple five-step process that helps you become aware of this energy and create a direct link for receiving it into your life.

Universal life-force energy is everything, is in everything, and is the energy that gives life. It exists outside of the intellectual mind, yet many of us need a way to wrap our minds around what this energy is and define what it means to us. Throughout human existence, life-force energy and universal life-force energy have been associated with the spiritual and divine. This need to categorize, personalize, anthropomorphize, and deify this energy continues today, as it always has, in both science and religion. Religious doctrines tell us that this energy is divine, and they give us names and forms to honor, worship, and follow, such as God, Jesus Christ, Allah, Jehovah, Shiva, and Buddha. Many of the indigenous spiritual and healing practices from around the world are being revitalized and disseminated, associating this energy with names such as the Goddess, Great Spirit, Chi, Prana, and Universal Power. Many traditions attribute this spiritual energy to powerful allies sometimes referred to as Angels, Ascended Masters, or Spirit Guides.

In chapter 6, you will learn that Western scientists and physicists are now referring to universal life-force energy as "the Mind of God," and philosophers and research psychologists are describing the personal identification with this spiritual energy as aspects of personal mythology. Practicing counselors and psychologists think of universal life-force energy as our religious belief system or personal higher power. We will learn how and why this is important. You will experience the benefits and power of universal life-force energy in its spiritual and divine aspects through activities designed to directly connect you with the Deities and Spirit Guides of your choice.

As explained earlier, before universal life-force energy differentiated into its varying structures, it was a formless, creative, conscious force called source energy. This omnipresent force created and permeates all energy and life, including you. Chapter 7 guides you to return to the pure state of source energy. I will explain how and why this benefits you, and demonstrate powerful activities that will help you release the boundaries that separate you from this dynamic power.

Energy for Life will fill you with vitality and diminish the energy draining patterns that deplete your enthusiasm and impede your ability to participate fully in your life. The only way for that to happen is for you to practice the energizing activities regularly. Chapter 8 is filled with easy and practical methods to help you incorporate energizing activities in your everyday life.

Remember, the activities you will experience in *Energy for Life* are the same ones I used to heal myself and re-energize from chronic illness and fatigue. From personal experience, I can attest, if you remain committed, you will connect with this powerful energy often and remain engaged throughout your daily life. You will become energized and miracles will happen!

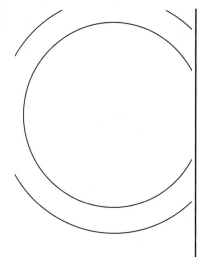

ONE

Energy 101

*To a mind
that is still
the whole universe
surrenders.
- Chuang Tzu*

WHAT IS ENERGY?

Energy is everywhere around us and in us at every single moment. It has been since the beginning of time, and will be until its end. We can easily see and feel many different kinds of energy—the power of an earthquake, a lightning flash, the glow of our ceiling light when we hit the switch, or a warming fire crackling in the grate—but we can't immediately define many forms of energy. The power of thought, the impact of emotion, and the magic of charisma are all observable but indefinable. Simpler yet, we know an apple as a food source. That's energy for our bodies. At the same time, the apple is full of seeds, which are little powerhouses teeming with enough potential energy in each one to produce an entire tree. It's easy for us to observe objects or phenomena, but we hardly ever regard the energies that drive them, make them up, and surround them.

With so much energy in and around us, why is it then that so many of us are disconnected from energy in its myriad forms? More importantly, how can we find and tap in to energy for our daily lives? And what exactly is this energy we are looking for, anyway?

We live in a radiant universe that moves and glows and interacts as it continually unfolds. Anything that we can sense or observe is, at its core, energy. There is no question that this energy takes different forms and has different characteristics in these varied forms. Heat, light, motion, electromagnetism, gravity, and the host of nuclear and quantum forces are all energies that we can observe. But where did *they* come from?

In the course of the last century, Western science has gone a long way to define and categorize the nature and wonder of these energies. As they have done so, they have begun to affirm what some of the most ancient belief systems in the world have made clear for millennia: The universe is nothing *but* energy. In fact, Einstein's equation $E=mc^2$ implicitly states that anything that has mass—meaning all matter, however great or small, dense or light—can be defined as energy.

The curious and interesting thing about our universe, though, is that it continues to become more and more complex over time. Astrophysicists claim that at one time, prior to the Big Bang, the entire universe consisted of a monochromatic ball of ultra-dense energy. Nothing else existed anywhere. As the Big Bang explosion took place, energy was disbursed in every direction and slowly began to differentiate and form the building blocks of stars and galaxies and the legion of energies and differing forms of matter we see today. After the Big Bang, there was a substantial period of time before our sun even winked into existence. Now our sun leads an entire system in which our Earth, once just a rocky ball in space, teems with trillions of creatures interacting within its biosphere. What can possibly be driving that kind of generative development?

In our world, we are constantly seeing things fall apart. It's almost a cliché. But something, some force or energy, over vast eons of time, is making things come together and become more complex instead of diminished. How can it be that this energy makes stars blaze with heat and light and promotes cosmic dust to coalesce to form planets that sail around the fiery sun? How then does that energy shape itself into elements like carbon, oxygen, and nitrogen, and form environments and chains of molecules that over time manifest life? Most importantly, how and why does that energy one day organize itself well enough to open its eyes, look around, and wonder where it came from and what it actually is?

It seems clear that some form of proto-energy is driving this syntropy, this building and evolving, over time. We can further observe that as this energy drives these phenomena, the end products of this evolution are becoming more and more self-aware. As we unlock the tools that help us understand the drive and goal of this proto-energy, we find that we are densified energy discovering the nature of itself. We have become a link in that generative chain. Our awareness of the energies that surround us, and how to understand and employ them for our benefit, is the next step in the overall evolution of awareness in this universe.

The first question of this awakening is: "Who and what am I?"

The answer: "You are densified energy moving about in a sea of other, subtler energies."

The second question then becomes: "How can I learn how to observe and utilize these gross and subtle energies in and around me to benefit myself and the universe?"

The answer is this book. Let's get started.

A Brief History

Although there are no written records, it seems clear that the earliest humans understood the fundamentals of energy. Archaeological evidence and early cave paintings indicate that water, wind, earth, and fire all figured prominently in the daily lives of the people of prehistory. The one other fascinating thing in these records is the presence of the unseen. It would appear that, from the earliest humans, our species had an instinctual understanding that there are unseen forces at work. As early people organized into groups, then tribes, then civilizations, they evolved their explanations of the unseen to fit the context of their own level of development.

Ancient texts, teachings, and practices reveal that every culture, tradition, religion, and spiritual path has (or had) at its root an understanding that energy is the force of life. Many of our ancient roots regarding energy are found in the practice of *shamanism*. Shamanism has always been a bridge between what is seen and what is unseen, and is a path whose deepest core belief is *animism*. Animism is the understanding that all things are living, connected and interconnected by an energy force called the *web of life*. All of manifest existence has a soul and a spirit—plants, animals, birds, this book, the chair you are sitting on, and you and me. Shamanism represents the most widespread and ancient methodological system of energy healing known to humanity, and is thought to have predated and been incorporated into all spiritualities and religions. This means that all of our great spiritual and religious traditions have at their base an understanding that everything is energy.

About four thousand years ago, ancient sages began to refine and document a practice of introspection that had sprung from rituals of this prehistoric shamanism. The transcendent nature of energy was discovered when the ancient sages began to analyze the nature of consciousness. Insights gained from these practices explained the forces of nature and the nature of the self in terms of energy. These ancient sages, the Vedics of the Indus valley in India, clearly drew on their traditional shamanic beliefs and combined these animist beliefs with their research into their own bodies, minds, souls, and spirits. The result was one of the most luminous texts ever produced—the Rig Veda. This text explained the seen and unseen as proceeding from a common genesis. That genesis was pure, high-powered, intelligent universal life-force energy. The Vedics claimed that this energy, pregnant with potential and driven to create, is the *fundamental* engine of creation. The products of this creation are the universe and everything in it, having been built by combining densified elemental energies into more complex structures. The upshot of all this is that the divine source energy, in its drive to create, formed an energetic structure as a background to the universe upon which all of manifest existence dances. According to the Rig Veda, this divine, blind impulse densifies and evolves, moving across the web of life, until it can find its way back, aware of itself this time, to the formless divine. Like the prodigal son in the Christian parable, the return of this self-aware energy, full of its acquired understanding, is cause for great celebration in the Vedic celestial spheres.

This concept of descent and rebirth is probably the most common mythical element in the history of mankind. It seems to be hard-wired right into our DNA. Every major mythology in the world includes it. The Hebrew Qabala reflects this energetic descent and return. Christian convention addresses the descent into purgatory accompanied by the ultimate rebirth into heaven. Taoist and Buddhist teachings reflect an awakening from a dull sleep into vibrant awareness. Sufism speaks rapturously of a reintegrating reunion with the divine after a descent into this world. Every one of these presents a methodology for how to bring this transformation about. Each has its own set of ideas about how to improve and enhance those personal attributes it considers valuable, and how to minimize those characteristics that diminish us. In other words, nearly every belief system in the history of the world presents a method for how to become lighter and brighter and power-filled in a world that seems full of things that drain and darken. They each give us recommendations about how to best utilize the energy we have and how, with practice, to dip into the infinite well of divine energy.

Each of these belief systems calls this divine energy by a different name. Each calls the energy in each of us by a different name as well. For the purpose of simplification, in this book we will call this energy in us "personal energy" or "personal life-force energy," and we will call the permeating energy "universal life-force energy." As you read this book, feel free to substitute whatever terms for personal and universal life-force energy that you use normally in your personal belief system. The terms are relatively unimportant. It's the concepts and practices that will be most beneficial to you in this process. Chapter six will guide you in how to utilize this information within the context of your individual religious or spiritual belief system. No matter the name, the energy is already there, just waiting for you to find it.

Modern Trends

With the advent of relativistic physics and quantum mechanics, we have begun to see that, on a quantum level, the boundaries between matter and energy are nonexistent. Even more interesting is that scientists are beginning to address the interconnectedness of being. Experiments demonstrating action at a distance as an effect of personal intent are becoming commonplace. In particular, the thought experiments of physicist John Wheeler have demonstrated that light leaving a distant star over a billion years ago will move through space *according to the expectations of the observer*. More and more, we are seeing that our thoughts and intentions influence outcomes in these experiments and in our lives. Heisenberg, with his famous uncertainty principle, established that the mere act of observation affects outcome.

Something on the quantum level is reacting to us. Something just outside of what can be observed is interacting with us as we interact with the world. What could that be?

In *Ageless Body, Timeless Mind*, Deepak Chopra states, "Quantum physics tells us that every atom is more than 99.9999 percent empty space, and the subatomic particles moving at lightning speed through this space are actually bundles of vibrating energy . . . [bundles that] carry information . . . . The essential stuff of the universe, including your body, is non-stuff, but it isn't ordinary non-stuff. It is thinking non-stuff. The void inside every atom is pulsating with unseen intelligence."[1]

Science is leading us to that island of realization the Vedics spoke of four thousand years ago. They are bringing us in line with the idea that our world is not only made up of energy—it is made up of an energy that is connected, interconnected, aware, and intelligent. The world and all of its forms are much more than the physical manifestations that we *see*. The energy that moves through all forms makes a tree more than wood and a person much more than just a body.

Kirlian photography has demonstrated a "halo" of energy that surrounds our bodies. This halo of energy flows around us and in us and is often seen as a multilayered "egg" that envelopes our bodies. These layers are parts of us that vibrate on higher, subtler levels. They constitute our intelligent energy field that interacts with the intelligent world of energy around us.

Energy Awareness

If intelligent energy is everywhere around us, why don't we know about it and perceive it in some way? Unless you are a scientist, engineer, or energy worker, you probably don't think much or know much about *any* kind of energy because you were not taught to be aware of it. In actuality, we do observe energy every day though we are usually unaware that the things we see, hear, and feel are gross and subtle manifestations of energy being perceived by our personal energy field. We don't come with built-in electron microscopes, but we do come with ultra-powerful, built-in energy receptors: our senses and energy field. Automatically, and most often unconsciously, our senses pick up extremely detailed information through seeing, hearing, feeling, knowing, and sensing.

---

1. Deepak Chopra, *Ageless Body, Timeless Mind: The Quantum Alternative to Growing Old* (New York: Harmony Books, 1993).

Energy is active, dynamic, and vibrating. The speed at which energy is vibrating determines if we can perceive it, how we will perceive it, and what it will look and feel like. Because *we* are also energy, the vibrations of energy outside of us interact with the vibrations of our personal energy field, causing us to sense this energy even though our five conventional senses might not register it. Our energy fields are amazing energy perceivers, receivers, and conductors, and it is through our senses that we receive the cognitive messages that something is happening that we can notice if we so choose. We could not possibly keep track of the unimaginable quantity of continuously flowing vibrations that we assimilate daily, but there are many that we do notice and more that we can train ourselves to notice to help us become healthier and more energized. The activities throughout this book and CD will help you become an aware perceiver, receiver, and conductor of energy.

Now that you understand energy on a bigger level, let's explore some of the ways that most of us perceive energy on an individual basis. The truth is, most people live their lives with blinders on. They see only what is in front of them, or the intensely personal landscape that they paint inside their minds. They don't notice what's going on around them. They don't taste what they eat or even notice what they touch. Most of us have become so focused on what we are doing, have done, or will do, that we ignore almost all of our sensory input in the present moment. In most cases when we do this, we are disconnected from our environment, our world, our energy, and ourselves. This disconnection is the precursor to fatigue, imbalance, and illnesses both emotional and physical. In order to develop a sense of the broad spectrum of subtler energies, we first have to learn to fully engage the much narrower band of our conventional senses.

When was the last time you completely engaged another person and were totally present with that person, aware of everything he or she said to you, his or her body motions, his or her eye movements? When was the last time you actually paid complete attention to what you were eating, aware of the nuance of taste, the texture of the food, and the food's aroma? When was the last time you sat and really listened to music? Not while driving or working, but sat in a chair with eyes closed and listened, submersed in the music?

Opening up to sensory information and being aware of it is the initial and most important part of developing the broader energy awareness. Take time during the course of your day to "take it all in." Open yourself completely to what's going on around you, to what you are feeling, seeing, hearing, tasting. Then, push your unseen sense, your energy sense, to feel the edges of what you can't feel with the five conventional senses. Let's explore some of the ways we can do that.

DEEPENING AND EXPANDING OUR PERSONAL AWARENESS OF ENERGY

The most important thing to keep in mind as you experiment with sensory development is that in order to sense something completely, you must be completely present. This applies to people and situations as well as objects and places.

When you are talking with people, try being completely present with them. Don't be thinking about where you are going, what's for dinner, or anything else. Be entirely with *them*. Look at them. What are they wearing? Look at the colors and the textures of their clothes. Observe their faces, their eyes. What color are they? Do they look tired, rested? Take in their expressions, the movement of their hands and bodies. Listen intently to their voices. Listen to the timbre of the voices. Are their voices shrill and cracking, or smooth and melodious? Can you smell perfume or laundry detergent on them? Turn your awareness inward. How do you feel inside your body as you notice the nuances and spend time with them? Go deeper into your personal awareness. What and how do you feel within yourself, wearing your clothes, having your scent, and speaking with your voice? Engage all of your senses in the moment. You will be amazed, and possibly a little overwhelmed, at the amount of information you can take in.

Now feel the subtle energy in the exchange. Are they being emotional in any way? Can you sense their anger, excitement, pain, joy? Deeper yet, do they leave you feeling uplifted and happy, or drained and depressed? This is just one of the easy ways to develop senses in the present, both subtle and gross. You can apply this technique of intense presence with any object or situation you wish.

But what is the mechanism that transmits all of this sensory stimuli to us so that we are able to receive information at all? The second most important thing to keep in mind is that all of the sensory input you receive in the present moment is vibrational in nature.

In the physical world, light is a vibration. Sound also. Smell, touch, and taste are all induced on our sense receptors and transmitted to our brains through vibration. These vibrations are energies resonating at a certain frequency. Color, shading, and density determine the frequency of vibration that we perceive with sight. But there are some frequencies that we don't readily register with our eyes. Infrared and ultraviolet rays are outside our normal range of perception. Even so, we can utilize modern technologies to see into these bands of light.

In the same way, we can be trained with ancient technologies of energy perception to see the energy fields around the human body. Skilled seers and clairvoyants can see these multihued energies that surround us. They also see that life-force energy is crystal clear, radiant, and translucent, and takes on added color when blended with these personal energies or the energy fields of other things. Shamans in the Toltec tradition are trained to see the human energy field as a luminous egg that surrounds us. By observing the state and condition of the egg, these shamans are able to diagnose all kinds of problems a person might have, and then treat them.

The same is true with hearing. We have a normal range of hearing, but there are bands of frequencies both above and below this. The trained ear can hear much more than the untrained. In the same way, professionals, especially those in counseling and psychology, are trained to listen intently. A good one hears not only what is being said, but also what is being left unsaid. They not only hear it, but they can feel it. And this, strangely enough, is where the hard-wired senses overlap with the energetic senses, right here in the "felt sense."

Perhaps one of the most misunderstood skills we have for sensing energy is our felt sense. All of us feel energy, even though our brains may not understand that this is what is happening. With our tactile sense, we feel the gross energies of the elements of the world, like the heat of a campfire and the charged feel in the air just after a lightning storm. We feel the energies of our personal bodies through touch and movement, and perceive personal energy through feelings and emotions. Through this felt sense we are able to sense the energy of each other. As we develop this felt sense, which includes all of our sensory information along with feelings and emotions, we begin to make huge leaps in what we are able to perceive.

This is the kind of felt sense that enables us to perceive and receive vast amounts of energy. This amazing felt sense comes from our personal energy field and its ability to feel all other energy. When our personal energy field senses something that is important for us to pay attention to, we receive feelings that we may refer to as gut feelings, intuition, knowing, or a sixth sense. These feelings may be sensed in our mind, emotions, or body, but they come as a feeling that is not consciously created by our mind, emotions, or body. We will discuss personal energy and energy fields in the next chapter, but it is important to recognize this amazing built-in energy perceiver and receiver that connects us with all other energies and sends us useful information about these other energies.

For example, many of us know the "good vibe/bad vibe" designation of what we feel when we are around certain people or in certain places. We sense things, like "this place feels warm and comfortable," "you could cut the tension with a knife," or "that person feels cold and angry," even though no one has said a word. This is the energy of people, animals, places, and things that we are sensing. All things vibrate, and these vibrations are sensed and read by our energy systems; the results manifest as feelings that can guide us. Likewise, we send out energy vibrations that others feel and read. This energy exchange is clear when you consider your responses to meeting someone that you instantly don't like or are instantly attracted to. The effect is like a magnetic push or pull, repelling or attracting. This response does not happen in your head as a result of thought—it occurs in the felt senses of your body's energy field.

It is in this way that we interact with the interconnected web of life. We are sentient beings who feel and respond to the many energies around us, just as these other energies feel and respond to the many energies around them. But I'd like to take this one step further. As you recall at the beginning of this chapter, I stated that everything is energy created out of energy, that energy is omnipresent and is the undercurrent, the potential, and the basis of all things. Energy is also all non-things and the space within and between things. Because of this, we are all one. Though we may seem separate because we have slightly different rates of vibration that allow for minute variations, we are—at our core—beings created using the same energy. So while we are our own personal energy, we are also a part of the greater whole. The web of life that our ancestors spoke about is not only an interweaving of all energies. It is also the whole of all energies.

Plain and simple, what this means to you is that all you need to do to energize yourself is to become aware of and connect with the infinite well of energy that exists both inside and outside of you. Awareness of the subtle energies may be a difficult thing to comprehend at first. You need to develop your responsiveness skills and use all of your senses to feel them. This takes practice. Begin by trying this exercise in energy play. With palms open and hands relaxed, rub your hands together. After doing this for a few moments, slowly pull them apart, really sensing what you feel. Do you feel the heat and pull of the energy? It may feel rather sticky, making it subtly harder to pull apart. You may also feel the pulsing and tingling vibration of the energy. Another energy-sensing exercise is to hold one hand palm up and draw circles about a half an inch above the palm, using the index finger of the other hand, not touching the palm. Can you feel heat or a tingling outline of the circle?

The activities described throughout this book are designed to facilitate this same flow of energy throughout your body and energy field. You may feel the powerful energy right away as you perform these activities, or it may take time and practice for you to begin to notice an increase in awareness and ability to tangibly feel energy. Once energy sensitivities and connections evolve, it becomes possible to harness the power of this force to fully energize yourself.

Understanding the nature of energy is essential for being able to employ it for your benefit. Now that you grasp all of that in general, it's time to approach practical ways to connect with and productively utilize energy.

HOW TO CONNECT WITH ENERGY

The first step to connecting with energy is taking the time to make it happen. This can best be accomplished by setting aside at least fifteen to twenty minutes per day to practice the energizing activity of your choice. You won't get energized if you don't practice the exercises that connect you with energy. Make a special date with yourself, and keep this appointment every day to the best of your ability.

The second step of your energizing program is to purchase or make a journal. This is an important step and one that should not be skipped, as journaling is a great tool for self-awareness and connection to energy. Find or make a journal that reflects your personality with pictures or designs that bring you energy. You will be using your journal to explore yourself, and this should be perceived as a fun tool. Perhaps for the first time in your life, you are giving yourself permission to take the time to explore yourself.

By taking a short amount of time each day after your guided journey, meditation, or energy connecting exercise to freely express yourself, you begin to reveal the deep, inner you that has been hidden under all the "doing" and all the roles you have to fill. Enjoy this special time that you get to spend with yourself, and allow this to be a time for self-nurturing and energizing. Write freely, and do not be concerned with grammar or punctuation. I want to emphasize again that this is not a trivial exercise. Through the process of journaling, you begin the process of re-acquaintance and communication with an old friend. Your journal entries help you to verbalize your experiences and therefore ground them in your body. You'll be amazed at the wisdom that will spring forth after immersing yourself in energy.

Guided Journeys

Each chapter contains a guided journey with pleasant visualizations and gentle suggestions that will soften and relax your mind and body into an altered state of consciousness. This state helps you access and sense energy more easily, especially at first. All of the guided journeys begin with the Universal Induction on page 18, so you may want to mark that page for easy reference.

The journeys can be read and then followed in your mind. Alternately, you can self-record the journeys so that your mind will be free to deeply relax as you follow along. You can also do them with a partner so that one can read the journey as the other performs it, then switch. To record your voice or to read for another, speak in a slow, soft monotone, pausing at all punctuation, and any other time you feel would be appropriate. Speak slowly and quietly. The object is for you or your partner to be lulled into deep relaxation.

The guided journeys, whether self-recorded, read by a partner, or from the accompanying CD, should never be listened to while driving a car or operating machinery. The intent of the induction is to guide you into a relaxed, altered state of consciousnesses that sets aside the conscious critical mind. This should be done only when you are in a safe and appropriate place.

Before each journey begins, you will be asked to ease yourself out of your everyday conscious mind by entering a space where you can relax and be comfortable, a place I call a "soft space." A soft space is a place where you feel calm, content, and at ease. This setting may vary depending on personal needs and tastes. Some people prefer airy, sunny rooms with fountains bubbling nearby. Some may prefer a cozy corner room in the basement painted in earthy tones, dimly lit, with soft drumming in the background. The place that you choose is a special place because it is where your energy resonates. If there is no such place in your home, perhaps there is a place in your vicinity—a meditation center, a reading room in the library, or a private room in your church. The place is of no consequence, but how you feel there is. Once you have found or created your soft space, I recommend taking a few minutes of quiet, alone time before beginning the guided journey. Try playing some relaxing or instrumental music to help you unwind, and then begin when you are ready. In this more relaxed state of consciousness, you will be more receptive to feeling, visualizing, and sensing the type of energy described in each guided journey.

Energy Meditations

In each chapter, the guided journey is followed by a meditation and several energy connecting exercises. The meditation is best undertaken during quiet, alone time when you are relaxed and comfortable. Each meditation will help you ponder the ideas addressed in that chapter and tap into your own inner wisdom about this type of energy and how you can best utilize its power. You don't need any knowledge of or experience with meditation. You need only to be willing to become aware of the energy and wisdom that is already flowing through you.

Begin each meditation by sitting comfortably in quiet contemplation in nature or in a soft space where you will not be disturbed. The intention of this type of meditation is nontraditional. You are not attempting to empty your thoughts and feelings by focusing on your breath or an object such as a candle flame as in many traditional forms of meditation. Your intention is to sink down into your thoughts and feelings, and really think and feel them while being fully aware of what you are thinking and feeling. Strive to be fully present with yourself during this practice. Do it with your awake and aware mind, emotions, body, and spirit. Be conscious in your head and in your heart with your feelings and emotions, with the sensations in your body, and with the vibrations and resonance of your energy field. Think about, wrap your mind around, sit with, and notice what you think, feel, and sense everywhere in your whole being about the subject of your meditation.

Then drop your awareness deep into your center to meet your inner wisdom. Your inner wisdom is the aspect of yourself that is your inner guide, your intuition and inner knowing. Here is where your body receives messages from your personal energy field in the form of the felt sense. Allow all the messages of your inner wisdom and felt sense to bubble up into your awareness. Be conscious of the felt sense every-where in your body. Notice what you feel physically. Be conscious of the felt sense everywhere in your mind. Notice everything that you are thinking. Be conscious of the felt sense everywhere in your emotions. Notice everything that you are feeling. Be conscious of the felt sense everywhere in your energy field. Notice what you feel spiritually. Notice what you feel intuitively. Become conscious in your whole being.

When you are ready, allow yourself to gently return to full ordinary consciousness. Take a few moments to notice what you feel with all your senses, thoughts, and emotions. You don't have to do anything with these feelings—just notice them. Become aware of what remains the same, and of any changes that you may sense. Write down your thoughts and feelings in your journal, fully expressing yourself as deeply and openly as possible.

Energy Connecting Exercises

The energy connecting exercises have been carefully designed to help you connect with energy all throughout the day with powerful results. They are also intended to help you awaken to your felt sense, become aware of the type of energy addressed in each of the chapters, and help you to perceive, receive, and conduct that type of energy. By using focus, intention, attention, visualization, and the physical gathering of energy, you will be able to connect with energy mentally, emotionally, physically, and energetically every day for the rest of your life.

The energy connecting exercises can be performed anywhere, at any time, because you do not need to enter into an altered state of con-sciousness for them to be effective. Each of these exercises is designed with a specific energizing purpose, be it igniting your personal energy, clearing blockages and leakages, or drawing in powerful universal, divine, and source energies. They are all superb energizers and fatigue busters. These exercises can be performed quickly wherever you are and whenever you are in need; or, if you have the time, the desire, and are in an appropriate place, you may choose to enter into an altered state of consciousness before performing these exercises for added relaxation and receptivity.

Connecting with Energy through Altered Consciousness

Intentionally relaxing your mind and body into a state of altered consciousness is a powerful way to become open and receptive to energy, especially for the beginner. Why? Because our ego-oriented, "ordinary" consciousness is often the very thing that blocks us from making a deep connection. To tap in to our personal and universal energies, we need to circumvent our everyday grocery-list mentality and speak to our self to incorporate the very seat of our being into our program of vibrant health and self-actualization. By setting aside our well-stratified psychological defenses and opening to a more fluid and less guarded energetic state, we initiate a positive move toward balance, openness, and overall clarity. Techniques for accomplishing this have been developed in a host of different psychological and spiritual disciplines the world over for millennia. They work by setting aside or getting underneath our cluttered, everyday ego-mind, often by inducing brainwave patterns most conducive to this outcome.

There are many effective ways to achieve an altered state of consciousness, such as progressive relaxation, visualization, and hypnosis, and indeed entire books have been written on these subjects alone. Entering into an altered consciousness occurs naturally through many methods, including such skills as daydreaming, lucid dreaming, becoming mesmerized by such things as a campfire, deep relaxation, countdown, prayer, meditating, journeying, trance dancing, drumming, rattling, and many forms of ritual and ceremony. Though entering into an altered state of consciousness is easy and natural, it may require patience if you are not accustomed to intentionally entering into such a state. It does become much easier with continued practice. When in this state, you will feel relaxed, yet aware, because your senses are heightened. You are always in control while in an altered state and can return to ordinary consciousness whenever you are ready simply by opening your eyes and reorienting yourself.

The Universal Induction described below is an effective tool for generating an altered state of consciousness through deep relaxation. By inviting the brain to become a distant observer, you create a calm, clear mind that allows energy to become more accessible. Whenever you have the additional few minutes needed, I recommend using this Universal Induction as a relaxation aid to start off any of the activities taught throughout this book. The Universal Induction is included on the accompanying CD as it is written here.

Universal Induction

Go to a soft space where you will be undisturbed, darken the room, and turn off all phones. Play any soothing, relaxing music that you enjoy. Sit or lie down where you will feel warm and comfortable, safe and protected. Take a moment to quiet yourself. When you are done with the induction, remain relaxed and quiet for as long as you are able, or have time for, and when you are ready to return, count back from twenty-one to one, slowly open your eyes, and allow yourself time to shift consciousness.

Take in a deep breath and relax. Allow your eyes to naturally close. Let go of any worries or stresses. Know that right now, there is nowhere else to go and nothing else to do. Relax and enjoy this time for yourself. Take in another long, deep breath, and feel the air expand and nurture your lungs. As you exhale, allow all of your stresses and tensions to release. Inhale again. With each inhalation, feel clear, pure energy entering your lungs and spreading throughout your body. With each exhalation, feel any toxins, discomfort, or pain exiting your body with the breath. Allow your mind to relax as the muscles of your body melt deep into the place where you are sitting or lying. Feel supported and cradled by the earth, floor, chair, couch, or bed. With your next inhalation and exhalation, allow your body to fully relax, feeling at peace. Allow any thoughts to flow through you, acknowledge them, and then let them float away, drift-

ing away like balloons high into the sky. Your mind relaxes and your brain becomes a quiet, distant observer.

As you continue to relax, a gentle, soothing feeling of relaxation washes up over your body and washes back down again, like a gentle lapping of waves. Relax and feel the rhythm of relaxation wash in, and wash back out, wash in, and wash back out, wash in, and wash back out. Warming, soothing, and relaxing.

As you continue to relax, resting in this peaceful, comfortable place, allow the muscles in your toes, feet, and ankles to relax. Feel those muscles as they lengthen and unwind, loosen and relax. Allow the muscles in your shins, calves, knees, thighs, and entire legs to become loose and relaxed.

As you continue to relax, allow the muscles in your pelvis, buttocks, stomach, and lower back to become loose and relaxed. All the muscles in your torso lengthen and unwind, loosen and relax.

As you continue to relax, allow the muscles in your chest, upper back, and lungs to become loose and relaxed. Feel those muscles lengthen and unwind, loosen and relax. Take in a deep breath, and feel the air filling your lungs, moving all the way down to the bottom of your lungs, pushing your belly out. As you exhale, push your stomach in to exhale all the way from the bottom of your lungs. Feel the air coming out through your nose and mouth. Feel the life-force energy of the breath move within you as you fully exhale and deeply inhale once more.

As you continue to relax, allow the muscles in your shoulders, arms, elbows, forearms, hands, and fingers to become loose and relaxed. Feel those muscles as they lengthen and unwind, loosen and relax. Allow the muscles in your neck, throat, face, the back of your head, and the top of your head to become loose and relaxed. Feel those muscles lengthen and unwind, loosen and relax. Take in a deep and satisfying breath, filling your lungs all the way down to your stomach, and as you release the breath, your body feels totally relaxed, loose and relaxed. Relax every muscle fiber and every nerve, totally relaxing your body, totally relaxing your mind.

As you continue to relax in this peaceful, comfortable place, soothing and healing and resting, deepen your relaxation and enter an altered state of consciousness by slowly counting in your mind from one to

twenty-one, relaxing deeper and deeper with every number that you
count. One, two, three, four, five, six, seven, eight, nine, ten, eleven,
twelve, thirteen, fourteen, fifteen, sixteen, seventeen, eighteen, nineteen,
twenty, twenty-one . . . deeply and totally relaxed. Allow yourself to drift
into a deep inner stillness.

After returning, with all your senses, thoughts, and emotions, take a few moments to notice what you feel. You don't have to do anything with these feelings—just notice them. Become aware of what remains the same, and of any changes that you may sense. Write down your thoughts and feelings in a journal, fully expressing yourself as deeply and openly as possible.

HOW TO USE THE CD FOR MAXIMUM BENEFIT

The accompanying CD is a powerful energizing tool consisting of five activities that vary in length from approximately five to twenty minutes. The activities on the CD, also reproduced on the pages mentioned below, as as follows: the Universal Induction, on pages 18–20; a peaceful guided journey called Sacred Healing Medicine Place, on pages 105–107; and three energy connecting exercises, including the Rainbow Waterfall on pages 63–64; the Lighted Energy Egg, on pages 93–94; and the Advanced Rainbow Fountain, on pages 167–172.

The Universal Induction is a guided relaxation that will gently ease you into an altered state of consciousness to help you access, sense, and receive energy more easily. It can be used by itself or in combination with any of the meditations or energy connecting exercises. Listening to the Universal Induction on the CD prior to practicing any of the activities will facilitate a stronger and deeper energy connection. Each of the three energy connecting exercises on the CD is designed with a specific energizing purpose, be it activating your personal energy, clearing blockages and leakages, or drawing in powerful universal, divine, and source energies. They can be practiced individually or in combination with each other and the Universal Induction. The guided journey, the longest activity on the CD, is a relaxing excursion that immerses your soul in the powerfully healing, high-vibrational energy of the universal life-force.

Used as a part of a consistent energy connecting practice and any time you need a boost of energy throughout the day, this CD will help open you to new worlds of energy.

. . .

Now that you understand the basics, you are ready to energize yourself. I invite you to engage your focus and intent, step into your power, and use the tools presented in this book and CD to enhance the vitality of your body, mind, and spirit. The energies of the universe are literally at your fingertips. All you have to do is claim this energy for life!

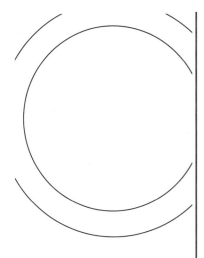

TWO

Connect
with Personal
Energy

*An energetic person has a sparkling rainbow
personal energy field that radiates brightly
from within and around their body.*
~ Colleen Deatsman

WHAT IS PERSONAL ENERGY?

Our personal energy sparkles and swirls through layers, wheels, and meridians forming a field of life and vitality. This amazing phenomenon is best understood when experienced firsthand. Join me on a journey into your personal energy field where you will see and feel for yourself the wonders of this force.

Close your eyes, take in a deep and satisfying breath, filling your lungs all the way down to your stomach, and, as you release the breath, allow your body to feel completely loose and relaxed. As you continue to relax, imagine that your conscious awareness has become concentrated to the size of a single oxygen molecule. As this molecule of conscious aware-ness, you are on the outside of your body, looking back toward your body. You brush up against your face and feel the softness of your skin. As this molecule, you are outside of your mind, emotions, thoughts, and feelings. In this place outside the body, you have no conscious awareness of what is going on inside your body and mind. You can't feel any pain or any pleasure. There are no emotions. You can't feel any sadness or any joy. There are no thoughts; just quiet awareness.

You begin to notice a gentle movement surrounding your body that has a rhythmic, flowing motion. At first, the movement seems random; then it appears to be organized, as if it has an intelligence of its own. As you look away from your body, you see a luminescent egg containing the movement flowing around your body. You sense its texture, and it feels soft and warm, light and electric. You recognize that this is your life-force energy pulsating around your body. It is your energy field, your aura. Sit with this for a while. Feel the movement.

Now let the movement of your breath carry you inside your body. You float in through your nose and enter into your lungs. You see and sense structures of the lungs, the bronchial tubes and the bronchi, the fibers and the cells, then the cells reduce to chains of molecules held together by some invisible force. Upon closer examination you see sepa-rate atoms that seem to have no matter at all. They appear to consist of swirling dots and minute contrails of light. At this atomic level of your-self you can sense the vastness and the intelligence of the space, and the sparks of energy that move through that space in each atom that forms each molecule that forms each cell that forms each system and organ, depending on the vibrational rate of the energy running through it. Allow your consciousness to stand in quiet observation of this amazing energy field that is the source and the force of your life. Feel the pulsation of your spirit and your energy. You are alive and glowing. Sit with this feeling and allow it to grow and circulate. Follow the flow of the energy as it moves out of your lungs, into and throughout your entire body, and then out beyond your body to encompass your whole being in a warm, pulsating glow of energy. Listen and feel as long as you can; then slowly and gently return to your ordinary consciousness.

We can understand viscerally from this experience what quantum physics and the world's philosophical, scientific, religious, and spiritual traditions have been teaching us. The universe and everything in it are made up of energy. Through the use of our imagination and senses we can feel in our own body and energy field the 99.9999 percent empty space in atoms. We can witness the subatomic particles flashing through them at lightning speed, and we can know and sense the innate intelligence of these vibrating energy bundles carrying the information that forms this energy into molecules, cells, and organized systems.

It is a miracle that our energy field is at once the essence of our life and the emanation of it, but that is only the beginning. Our personal energy field also organizes into a nurturing, protective conscious field that keeps us alive and connects us with other energies. This energy field is associated with heat and appears like flames or heat waves around a person. Aerospace scientist and energy healing school founder Barbara Brennan tells us in her book *Hands of Light*, "The Human Energy Field is the manifestation of universal energy that is intimately involved with human life. It can be described as a luminous body that surrounds and interpenetrates the physical body, emits its own characteristic radiation and is usually called the aura."[2] Throughout history, shamans, mystics, psychics, and intuitives have been able to see this energy and describe it as a radiant haze around the body.

Individuals with strong personal energy and those who cultivate their connections to life-force energy have a pronounced energy field that radiates brightly from within and around their bodies. This is often associated with a strong spiritual practice and is the observable light in depictions of avatars, saints, and spirit beings, such as angels and guides that appear to have halos encompassing their heads. We all have halos, though the intensity varies based on our ability to build and maintain our personal energy. You may recall feeling this energy while doing the simple energy sensory perception activities in chapter one.

Advancements in modern technology have given us amazing instruments with which to visibly measure, witness, and photograph the physical manifestation of personal energy. Kirlian photography can show us the energy halos that surround our bodies. Other sensitive scientific technologies such as nuclear magnetic resonance (NMR), computed axial tomography (CAT scan), and ultrasound are able to give us pictures of otherwise inaccessible internal organs by reading and interpreting minute energy signatures produced by stimulating the deep tissues.

These instruments tend to validate the great teachings of our ancestors, who long understood and honored our personal energy as the source and sustenance of life. Some of the most clear and concise teachings on the human energy field come from the Hindu Vedics, who tell us that a person is much more than just a body. In fact, the body turns out to be little more than an animate coat rack in the Vedic grand scheme of things. The "coat," as it were, consists of other coverings of energy and consciousness that surround and intermingle with our bodies. These coverings are what animate us.

In the most general terms, people have three energetic layers we know as gross, subtle, and causal. These correspond very roughly to what we would term body, mind, and spirit. Each of these three layers also has states and brain wave rhythms in which they naturally predom-

_____

2. Barbara Brennan, *Hands of Light* (New York: Bantam Books, 1987).

inate, namely when we are awake (beta), dreaming (alpha), in deep trance (theta), and in deep sleep (delta).

The body's domain is wakefulness, and serves as our physical force in the physical world. All the tools we need to interact with the world, including our egos and worldly identities, exist in the gross physical, waking state.

The mental/emotional/soul-self domain is the dream state, or alpha and theta states of consciousness. This is the subtle realm, and it is vast and layered. It encompasses the very simple, such as enthusiastic vitality and daydreaming, all the way up through the transpersonal, with expanded consciousness and archetypes, and on into absolutely amazing phenomena like intuition, precognition, and psychic awareness. In the subtle realms, we have experiences while we are completely dissociated from our bodies and egos. Here, anything is possible. We could be mermaid accountants on Mars in the dream state, and it will seem perfectly natural to us until we wake up and reassociate ourselves with our physical body and identity. This multilayered state is where we can first begin to perceive the energy that permeates the universe of form and all of us at every moment. This is life-force energy. In the subtle states, life-force energy is the do-er, the revitalizer. It is what we can tap in to to stay healthy, gain awareness, and manifest what we want in our lives. Life-force energy is the resident, permeating energy in the subtle realms, but its origins lie in the causal realm of spirit.

The spirit part of us dominates in the causal state of dreamless deep sleep. The ancients believed this to be our truest state. Here we swim in the vast ocean of timeless awareness free of all physical and mental constructs. This sea of consciousness is what exists before anything becomes manifest. This is the nondual Source, "the one without a second." It is said that we must make contact with this Source frequently in order to stay alive, whether we do it on purpose or not. That's why sleep is essential. It ushers us into the causal state and replenishes the higher aspects of ourselves with just enough of this fundamental energy to animate us. This causal state of being is where we overlap with all that is. We blend here with the eternal and are one with the pure potential of this nonmental, nonphysical reality. Universal life-force energy emanates from here in its purest, lightest form, and, as the first manifestation of the causal, is the background or vital undercurrent of all that is. As all matter is energy in different forms and densities, all energy is universal life-force energy manifesting in different ways and in differing densities. It is the unified field that is our personal energy field while at the same time being universal life-force energy. All of this energy collectively is the primordial intelligence that includes the web of life and influences all of manifest creation right down to the cellular level.

Looking deeper within these layers of our personal energy field, we see an intricate system of wheels, paths, and other layers that act as conduits and gateways of energy flow and exchange with all of the layers within ourselves, each other, and the world. Many systems employ slightly different terminology describing the nature of this energy flow, such as the Chinese with yin and yang flowing on the body's energy meridians, the energy chakras and auric layers of the Vedas, or the energy grid and sephiroth of the Hebrew Qabala.

Using Chakras to Connect with Energy

I find the Vedic system of chakra wheels and layers to be easy to understand and powerful to work with, so I utilize this concept to induce energy flow in some of the energy connecting exercises. Remember that this and all systems are merely models to help us understand and address the energies in and around us. Use this model as a guide and a tool, but leave yourself open to your own experiences and any intuitive information that you might receive during the course of performing the exercises here. The chakra wheels and layers are only briefly described below for ease of use and understanding. If you desire a more in-depth understanding, I highly recommend the book *Hands of Light,* by Barbara Brennan.

The chakra system consists of seven major and twenty-one minor spinning circles or wheels located in specific places in the body where the personal energy field exchanges energy with itself and the universe. Each major chakra has a corresponding auric layer around the body that also has seven major chakras. The auric layers are an integral part of the personal energy field, acting as energetic protection and conduits that pass energetic information through each concentric layer. The chakra energy centers circle through and around the body, moving up from the feet through the torso to the head and beyond, and are connected within the body by energetic pathways. Each chakra has a quality and frequency of energy that work to create and maintain balance in specific areas of the body and energy field.

There are those who work with only the seven major chakras; however, I prefer to work with twelve chakras: both feet, root, sacral, solar plexus, heart, palms of both hands, throat, third eye, crown, and universal. The first chakras are located in the arches of each foot and express a brownish-maroon color in the aura. They are associated with the term grounding, used to describe the conscious act of energetically connecting with the energy of Mother Earth.

The next chakra, referred to as the base chakra or root chakra and the first chakra in the seven major chakra system, is located at the base of the torso, behind and beneath the genitals in the groin area. This chakra typically expresses the color red. It is associated with our survival impulse, our quantity of physical energy, and our physical sense of touch. This chakra also helps us to ground with Earth energy and is associated with the first layer, called the ethereal body. Correlating organs are the adrenal glands, spinal column, and kidneys.

The feet and the root chakras make up the physical body and constitute the gross or physical layer.

The sacral chakra is located in the abdomen just above the pubic bone and encircles the hips. This chakra typically expresses the color orange. It is associated with quality of love and quantity of sexual energy. It is associated with the second layer, called the emotional body. Correlating organs make up the reproductive system.

The solar plexus chakra is located in the center of the torso above the navel and below the rib cage, circling around to the center of the back and around again to the front. This chakra typically expresses the color yellow. It is associated with personal will power, pleasure, spiritual wisdom, and being in the center of one's universe. It is associated with the third layer, called the mental body. Correlating organs are the pancreas, stomach, gallbladder, and nervous system.

The heart chakra is located in the rib cage at the heart, circling around between the shoulder blades and back around to the heart. It typically expresses the color green or pink. It is associated with love, compassion, and our actions in the physical world. The fourth layer, called the astral level is associated with this chakra. Correlating organs are the thymus, heart, vagus nerve, and circulatory system.

The chakras of the hands are located in the palm of each hand. Reiki practitioners will know these well, as they are the focal point of energy transmission during a healing session. These chakras typically express the color gold. The hand chakras not only express and send out energy, but they are also important vortexes for receiving. The hands connect us to the outside world and are very finely tuned energy sense organs.

What is commonly referred to as the fifth chakra in the seven chakra system, the throat chakra, encircles the neck. This chakra typically expresses the color blue. It is associated with one's sense of self, voice in the world, responsibility for self, and physical sense of hearing, taste, and smell. The fifth layer, called the etheric template layer, is associated with this chakra. Correlating organs are the throat, thyroid, and lungs.

The sixth chakra, or the third eye, is located in the forehead just above and between the eyes. This chakra typically expresses the color indigo. It is associated with visualization and mental and psychic understanding. The sixth layer, called the celestial body, is associated with this chakra. Correlating organs are the pituitary gland, lower brain, ears, and nose.

The sacral, solar plexus, heart, throat, hands, and third-eye chakras constitute the subtle layer.

The seventh chakra, or the crown chakra, is on top of the head and typically expresses the color violet. It is associated with one's connection to spirituality and integration of one's whole being. Correlating organs are the pineal gland and upper brain.

Little is known about the eighth chakra, which I refer to as the universal chakra. It is located above the head and is thought to be engaged when connecting with the high vibrations of the greater cosmos, universal powers, and spiritual truths of enlightenment. Many explorers into the causal realms believe that there are several higher chakras that can be experienced only after we graduate to a higher realm or level of vibrational awareness. The universal chakras are of a high vibrational rate that is electric, clear, and translucent.

The crown and the higher universal chakras make up the causal layer.

Inside of this system and many others, including Chinese medicine, Chinese astrology, modern astrology, African Dagara traditions, and Ayurveda, we find that energetically and physically we are made up of subtle, primal energies called elements. In physical chemistry, elements are the building blocks of molecules, compounds, cells, larger structures, and organisms. In energy disciplines, the fundamental elements are referred to as earth, air, fire, and water, and are the influences whose energies build the *characteristics* of things within the physical universe. Every physical object is a combination of these elements in unique proportion. So, just as physical elements combine to form our body, its structures, and thus the whole of us, these energetic elements combine to determine the characteristics of our body's systems, and ultimately the nature, or *flavor*, of our personal energy. As these elements form together, we become an organized system that is the physical manifestation of a combination of water, earth, air and fire. Not only does this combination create our physical being, but every day our physical and energetic bodies must interact with the gross *and* subtle forms of these same elements to sustain our life.

The very elements that are the building blocks that form our physical body and our energy field move through our physical body and energy field to keep our life-sustaining energy active and flowing. This internal and external flow of the elements keeps our energy dynamic and flowing and our physical body living, breathing, and feeling good. We know that, physically, we die within a matter of minutes without breathing air; without drinking water we die within a matter of days; and without the combustion of burning calories in a subtle form of fire to warm us, and earth to live upon, we would perish in short order. So as we explore layers, wheels, paths, and meridians of energy flow, we must also be aware that our energy field consists of *energetic* elements that must interact with each other inside of us, just like their physical counterparts, in order to sustain our vigor, vitality, and life.

The elements are so much a part of our energy field that we actually take on physical attributes of the elements in our body, mind, emotions, spirit, and personality. We all know people who we consider to be fiery; they seem to be full of energy, and we call them spark plugs. Those who are earthy seem to be calm and stable, whereas those who are watery tend to be emotional and intuitive, and those who are airy tend to be intellectual and good communicators. These "stereotypes" are simple generalizations intended to demonstrate the important energetic tendencies expressed by our energy field, which is governed by the rate of energy vibrations that make up the elemental "soup" of our energy field.

We are physiologically and energetically a combination of all of the elements. Historically, intricate systems have evolved that equate specific elemental tendencies with a person, depending on variables such as date and time of birth or conception. Most of these systems agree that we consist of the elements of earth, water, air, and fire. However, many systems work with a five-element theory and believe that we may also contain the elements of ether, mineral, metal, wood, or nature, depending upon the system. Perhaps all of these elements exist within us, perhaps not. Our purpose in this book is not to explore the elements and their tendencies that manifest in personality traits, but to utilize the tangible feelings that we already recognize and equate with specific elements to help us explore and balance our energy field. Because it is difficult for some to tangibly see, feel, and sense the invisible force of our energy field, working with the elemental aspects of energy can open the door to visceral sensation and understanding. Many of the activities in this book will guide you in this process.

Abundant vigor, vitality, health, and quality of life are dependent on harmonious, balanced, flowing energy. Since the elements, layers, and chakras of our energy field serve to protect and vitalize the body, an imbalance in the energy field ultimately creates an imbalance in the physical body that can manifest as low energy, fatigue, pain, or illness. Energy healing has been practiced globally throughout our history and has become more accepted and mainstream in the modern Western world. As more and more people become frustrated with the limitations of allopathic medicine, we are turning once again to the energizing and healing techniques of our ancestors. A body becomes fatigued and ultimately ill when it has fallen out of harmony and balance, and becomes energized and well again once balance and harmony are restored. Imbalance and disharmony are caused by inactive personal energy, disruptions in energy flow, such as blockages and leakages, and failure to connect with outside energies. Harmony and balance can be restored with techniques that bring energy into the body and move stagnant energy out of it. Many current methods of treatment handed down from our ancestors, such as acupuncture, therapeutic touch, and Reiki, are based on this very premise. The same effects can also be accomplished on your own by using techniques that invite energy flow throughout your body and energy field. We all have the ability to connect with and utilize energy, and the activities taught throughout this book will help you become a proficient self-energizer.

Connecting with, moving, and utilizing personal energy may be a new concept for modern Western society, though it is, and has been, a common practice worldwide in cultures where the importance of energy is understood. Seemingly miraculous stories are being shared out of the East, such as the remarkable youthfulness and vigor of the Yogis of India, who have been moving Prana since childhood, and Buddhist monks utilizing Chi to stay warm while meditating on mountaintops in subzero temperatures wearing only their everyday robes.

You may not be able to perform feats such as these until you become practiced and adept, but you will feel much more healthy, vital, and energetic by activating your own energy field. The activities described in this chapter will help you learn how to allow, guide, and stimulate your personal energy to reignite and flow with power that is energizing to mind, body, and soul.

Why Would I Want to Activate My Personal Energy?

Within your energy field right now lives all the power you need to create the vigor and vitality to live your life fully. Your personal energy field is a dynamic display of dancing energy vibrations that, when stimulated, will bring you vibrant health and plenty of energy to do anything you desire. This internal force, when balanced and flowing strongly, will make you look younger, feel younger, boost your immune system, help you sleep better at night, and feel calm and balanced emotionally, mentally, physically, and spiritually. Connecting with your personal energy is a powerful way to prevent fatigue and illness, and is a must to revitalize an already fatigued, ill, or weakened energy field.

How to Activate My Personal Energy

There are many effective ways to activate your personal energy. It is as simple as paying attention to and becoming aware of what is happening inside of yourself. When beginning, this is most easily accomplished when you slow down your busy conscious mind and become still. The following guided journey will help your mind and body relax as you are gently guided into an altered state of consciousness. While in this state you will access your personal energy field and begin to see, sense, and feel the flowing movement of your chakras, layers, and internal elements. This is followed by a meditation and several energy-moving exercises. All of these activities utilize the skills of mental focus, attention, awareness, mindfulness, visualization, and intention. Some of the exercises also include body movement.

GUIDED JOURNEY

Energize My Personal Energy

To be energized and completely healthy, one must activate, stimulate, and balance the wheels, layers, and elements of one's energy field. This guided journey will help you accomplish just that. Using the power of your intention and imagination, you will excite your energy field into a dynamic flow that will arouse your vitality, radiance, and gusto.

Go to your soft space where you will be undisturbed, darken the room, and turn off all phones. Play any soothing, relaxing music that you enjoy. Sit or lie down where you will feel warm and comfortable, safe and protected. Take a moment to quiet yourself, and allow yourself to become deeply relaxed using the Universal Induction.

As you continue to relax, allow yourself to see, sense, and feel the natural flow and rhythm of your personal energy surrounding your body. Notice the energy pulsating over the cells of your skin like soft ocean waves gently lapping each granule of sand at the water's edge. Feel the flow tenderly wash up your body, and wash back down, wash up your body, and wash back down, wash up your body, and wash back down, bathing each cell in its own tiny pool of nurturing energy. Now activate your personal energy by stirring each pool of energy surrounding each cell using your focus and intention. Feel the energy bubble up around each cell and around your whole body, as if you are immersed in the soothing waters of a hot mineral bath. Breathe deeply of your nurturing energy spa, and feel the warm glow and the exciting tingle of your own energy wrapped around you. On your next inhalation, tiny atoms of your energy spark in the air, enter into your lungs, and sink into the deep rich, earth of your body. The energy saturates every cell throughout your entire body. You see, sense, and feel the amazing powerhouse of energy within you. Allow it to move through you.

Feel your energy as it sinks down to the soles of your feet and tickles your arches. Stimulate the energy by spinning it around in your foot chakras. The energy warms as it moves up your legs and anchors itself into your root chakra at the base of your torso. As it circulates and spins at your base it begins to take on a deep ruby-red glow. Allow yourself to sense and feel the heat and the tingle. It continues to heat up as it moves to your sacral chakra in your abdomen and becomes a vibrant orange. Feel the spinning energy bring a warm glow to your tummy and lower back. The gathering heat moves the energy into your solar plexus and becomes a fiery yellow ball of inner sunshine at the base of your ribs. Feel the hot glow energize your center. As the swirling heat of your inner sun moves up into your heart chakra, the color transforms into a radiant mix of compassionate pink and healing forest green. Energy, heat, and compassion move upward into the throat chakra, where they take on the azure blue of speaking one's truth. Spin the blue wheel in your throat, and feel the power of your own energy and voice. Moving up into your third eye and crown chakras, the energy glows a velvety indigo that melts into effervescent violet. The excited energy opens a gateway inside your own energy field that allows you to see visions and connect with your inner wisdom. Allow yourself to see, sense, feel, and experience these visions, intuitions, and knowings for a few moments.

When you are ready, send the spinning energy up into your translucent eighth chakra and notice any sensations that you experience. From this place inside your energy field but just outside of your body, you can see that the dynamic energy you are experiencing moving up your body is also moving down, and around, and within, and through your body and the layers of your energy field simultaneously.

In a synergistic dance, the atoms, molecules, and cells of your body and energy field continually unite in a dazzling display of internal fireworks. Every moment of every day your own personal celebration is booming inside of you, exploding into beautiful pinwheels of rainbow colors that burst open with energy and shoot out throughout the entirety of your body and energy field. Feel this power electrifying every level of your being.

Feel it flow through every layer of your energy field. Feel it flow deep into the watery rivers of your being and sink into the earthy matter of your body, drenching every cell, molecule, and atom of your being in excited energy. See, feel, and sense the tingling, sparkling energy move through your physical body and instantly flow from the inside out, back into the layers of your aura, energizing and refreshing your whole being.

Take in a deep breath, and feel your life-force energy deep within your body and soul. Feel the vibrations growing stronger and stronger within you, with every breath that you take and every beat of your heart. With each passing moment, your personal energy field becomes more pronounced *and flows more strongly. You feel full of vitality and get-up-and-go. You feel ready to live your life powerfully. You are energized!*

When you are ready, begin the process of returning to ordinary awareness. Slowly count from twenty-one to one, becoming more awake and more alert with every number that you count, being fully awake and alert at the number one. Gently feel yourself come back fully into your body, and open your eyes.

Sit quietly for a few moments and reflect on your experience. Be gentle with yourself as you wiggle and stretch, becoming fully present in your body and conscious mind. Document your thoughts and feelings in your journal.

MEDITATION

Perceive and Connect with Personal Energy

Sit in quiet contemplation in nature or in a soft space where you will not be disturbed. Open your mind and relax. Observe, notice, experience, and feel everything going on inside of you. Focus your attention on your feelings and opening up all of your senses to experience the personal energy moving inside of you. Allow any distracting thoughts to drift away. Notice them and let them go.

Continue to sit quietly, and observe yourself. See and feel, or imagine and feel, everything about yourself, inside and out. What do you sense outside of your body? What do you feel physically? What do you feel emotionally? What do you sense inside of your body? Is there any movement? What elements do you notice? Do any of the elements blend together? Relax, look deeper, and continue to observe for a while. Allow yourself to sense and feel everything about your personal energy, and then experience the space in between. Allow yourself to sense and feel all of your thoughts, and the empty space in between. Allow yourself to sense and feel all of your emotions, and the empty space in between.

Allow yourself to sense and feel the physical energy of your body, and the space in between. Allow yourself to sense and feel the energy that is all four, and then experience all the space in between. Breathe deeply of this energy. Notice your sensations.

Now close your eyes and allow your inner wisdom to bubble forth. Relax, focus, and feel. Open up to feeling all the energy moving around and through you. Allow questions and answers to form in and out of your thoughts, questions like: Does the combination of the elements affect my energy levels? Where are my energy wheels? Are they open and spinning? What am I feeling in the chakra locations? Is my personal energy my soul? Do I feel energy moving around and through me? Are there different layers of energy outside of my body? Can I feel these? Can I see these? What colors do I see, feel, or sense? What vibrations do I see, feel, or sense?

Stay in this place in contemplation for as long as you have time, asking your own questions of yourself. When you are ready, take in a deep breath and allow yourself a few moments to shift your awareness back to ordinary life and fully integrate back into your body. Write your thoughts and feelings in your journal.

PERSONAL ENERGY CONNECTING EXERCISES

The following exercises can be performed anywhere at any time. If you have the time and are in an appropriate place, you may choose to enter into an altered state of consciousness (as described in chapter 1) before performing these exercises for added relaxation and openness.

Chakra Opening/Connecting

Opening and connecting with the chakra energy centers of the body is a powerful exercise in recognizing and filling with energy. The Chakra Opening/Connecting exercise involves focusing all of your attention on each chakra one at a time, for several minutes.

Begin by closing your eyes. Take in a deep, relaxing breath. Allow your-self a few moments to disengage from your everyday life. When you feel ready, focus all of your attention and consciousness on the chakras in the arches of your feet. Relax and try to feel any physical sensations or emo-tions that are there. Relax and focus. Notice whatever is happening in your arches, in your feet, and any sensations that may be moving up your ankles and into your legs. Now move your body around a little bit to change your attention to your root chakra. Place all of your concentra-tion on this area of your body for a few minutes. Close your eyes, relax, and try to feel any physical sensations or emotions that are there. It may help you to place your hands on this area of your body to help hold your attention. Relax and focus. Connect with whatever is happening in this location of your body. Now move your body around a little bit to change your focus, and place your attention on your sacral chakra. Again, relax and try to feel any physical sensations or emotions that are there. Place your hands on your body if it helps your concentration, and connect with whatever is happening in this location of your body. When you feel ready, move a bit to change your focus and place your attention on your solar plexus. Continue this pattern through the remaining six chakras: heart, hands, throat, third eye, crown, and universal. Move slowly through each of the twelve chakras, relaxing and feeling any physical sensations or emo-tions that are present. Common sensations felt by doing this exercise are an increase in body temperature, euphoria, mental relaxation, and physi-cal energy.

Centering

Centering is a powerful energizing exercise that brings you back into bal-ance quickly. Often our energies are scattered, causing us to feel anxious and out of balance. When we stay "uncentered" for too long we leak energy and begin to feel tired. Centering brings all of your personal energy back home into your energy field and body.

*Take in a deep breath, close your eyes, and relax your mind and body.
Begin with your arms down beside your legs. Extend your arms out at
your sides, palms facing up. Slowly sweep them up while using the powerful intention of your mind to gather in your energy and thoughts from
everywhere around you, calling your energy back home to your energy
field and your body. See, sense, and feel your energy coming back from the
outer world into your energy field and into your body as your hands and
arms come up over your head. Draw your hands and arms down over
your head in front of your face and down the front of your body, bringing
your hands to rest on your solar plexus. Using all of your senses, really
feel the energy coming into your head, neck, shoulders, chest, and center.
Once you feel your energy settled in your solar plexus, pull it down far-
ther into your body with your hands and intention, anchoring it deep in
your root chakra. Repeat three times.*

Fill with Love

A variation of the Centering activity is the Fill with Love exercise. Perform the Centering exercise described above, and as you scoop your
personal energy and bring it into your body, solar plexus, and root
chakra, say out loud, "I Love Me, I Love Me, I Love Me!" Repeat three
times. Love is a powerful energy, and loving yourself stimulates your
energy field.

Personal Energy Boost

The Personal Energy Boost exercise helps you stimulate your personal
energy quickly.

*Begin by taking in a deep breath and relaxing. Place your hands just
above the top of your head, open palms down. Hold this position while
focusing the power of your mind on the color violet. You are open to feel-*

ing and receiving energy. After a few moments, move your hands down to cover your third eye (forehead) and the back of your head. Hold, focus on the color indigo, and feel and receive the energy. Move to your throat center, placing your hands just above the body in the front and back of your neck. Hold, focus on the color blue, and feel and receive. Move to your heart center, placing both of your hands on your chest. Hold, focus on the color green, and feel and receive. Move to the solar plexus, placing your hands on the center of your being. Hold, focus on the color yellow, and feel and receive. Move to the spleen center, placing your hands on your abdomen. Hold, focus on the color orange, and feel and receive. Move to the root center, placing your hands just above the body of your genital area and derriere. Hold, focus on the color red, and feel and receive. In one movement, take your hands to the floor and sweep up all of your personal energy with your hands open, fingers together, palms facing your body. Bring your hands all the way up your body from the floor to above your head while feeling and visualizing rainbow-colored energy. Feel and receive the energy flow.

Energy Circle

The Energy Circle exercise provides a discipline of moving life-force energy through the energy channels of the body. This technique is also known in India as "Opening the Kundalini."

Begin by placing your attention on your abdomen between your solar plexus and sacral chakra. This is known in many martial arts practices as your point of balance. When warmth builds (this is energy), move the warmth with mindful intent down to your root center at the base of your torso, resting it there for a few moments. Now move the warmth up the back of your body into your spinal cord, and allow it to rest for a few moments at your kidney point. Raise the energy slowly up your spine to the top of your head. Follow the energy flow without force.

Hold and rest the warmth at your crown chakra for a few moments. Now direct the energy flow down to your third eye (forehead), and flow it back down to your navel. Repeat this circle several times. When proficient, include your arms and legs. From your balance point, direct the energy flow to your root center, divide it into two channels, and send the energy down the backs of your legs to the arches of your feet, allowing it to rest there. Once warm, move the energy all throughout your feet and toes, then up the front of your legs to your shins, knees, thighs, and back to your root center. Return the flow up your spine, and then divide it into two channels at the point between your shoulder blades. Send the energy down the insides of your arms to the middle of your palms. Hold and rest, and then direct the energy down to your middle finger and back out along the backside of your arms, returning to your heart area, where the energy flows to your head, forehead, face, navel, and back to your balance point. Repeat several times. Be mindful. Notice what you feel.

This one is really high powered! If you feel nauseated while doing this, take in a deep breath and relax. Move the energy slowly. Practice will increase your body's ability to handle this powerful energy.

Inner Wisdom

Your Inner Wisdom is the aspect of your personal energy that is your inner guide, your intuition, and your inner knowing. Your mind is a powerful thinker and perceiver, and so is your energy field. This exercise will help you to quickly get in touch with these powerful sensations that we often call "gut feelings."

Close your eyes, take in a deep breath, and relax. Become quiet inside. Ask your energy, mind, emotions, soul, and body to "talk" to you. Listen . . . really listen. Hear, see, sense, and feel what is being communicated. Allow yourself to become aware of your inner knowings. Carry on a conversation with your inner wisdom and ask it to communicate with you. Give yourself permission to feel whatever you are feeling, and then challenge yourself to go even more deeply into your own internal wisdom. Be aware of anything that you notice. Ask your inner wisdom if there is any other information that you need to be aware of, and wait for the response. When you are ready, thank yourself, take in a deep breath, and open your eyes. Write down your knowings, thoughts, and feelings in your journal.

Inversion Awareness Energy

The Inversion Awareness Energy exercise harnesses the power of your mind to become aware of, draw in, and utilize the powerhouse of energy that is already flowing through your personal energy field.

Step 1: *Sweep all of your personal and mental energy inside of yourself. Begin by taking in a deep breath and closing your eyes if you choose. Shake off the stresses of the day with a gentle shaking of your body. Allow your mind to relax and focus inward. Extend your arms out at your sides, palms facing up, and sweep your arms up over your head. Pull your personal energy from all the layers of your energy field outside of yourself down to the inside of your head. Blend your personal energy with your consciousness, concentration, attention, intention, and mental energy. Pull all of this energy in through your head and neck and into your heart chakra. Hold the energy here, and be aware of the vibrations and feelings it brings. Hold for a while. Feel and sense your energy and feelings. When ready, pull it down deeper into your center and hold it. Feel, sense, and be aware of the vibrations and the wisdom it brings.*

Step 2: *Sweep the energy of your internal sun inside of yourself. Your internal sun resides in your third chakra and in the third layer of your energy field. It appears as a bright yellow light radiating around your body. Extend your arms out at your sides, palms facing up, and sweep your arms up over your head. With your intention, pull in the illuminating* power of your energy field sun down inside of your body. Pull this radiant energy in through your head and neck and into your heart chakra. Hold the energy here, and allow the light to illuminate your emotions and feelings, shedding light on the awareness and insights felt in step 1. Hold for a while. Feel. Sense. When ready, pull it down deeper into your center and hold it. Allow the light of your energy sun to illuminate your wisdom and your entire energy field. Hold for a while. When ready, anchor your personal energy and the energy of your sun into the base of your body at your root chakra and see, sense, and feel the energies blending into a radiant, swirling rainbow.

Step 3: Bridge this energy from bottom to top by sending swirling, rainbow, sparkling electric energy from chakra to chakra up your spinal column and body from your root chakra to your center. Hold. When ready, send swirling, rainbow, sparkling electric energy up your spinal column and body from your center to your heart chakra. Hold. When ready, send swirling, rainbow, sparkling electric energy up your spinal column and body from your heart chakra to your head. Hold. Feel the power! Sense the energy!

Step 4: When the internal bridge is complete, expand the swirling, rainbow, sparkling electric energy from the core of the inside of your body out into your whole energy field, inside and outside of your body. Hold. Feel the power! Sense the energy!

Continue the energy flow for as long as you have time, and then write your sensations, feelings, and thoughts in your journal. When you are finished, gently return your focus to your ordinary world.

· · ·

If I could see you now, and you have been doing the activities in this chapter, I would see a person with a sparkling rainbow personal energy field that radiates brightly from within and around his or her body. Hopefully, you have a lot of energy and are feeling vital and healthy. Stimulating one's own energy field goes a long way in harnessing power, vigor, and dynamism. Sometimes, though, even when we are diligent in our energy connecting and moving practice, other factors such as energy blockages and leakages influence our ability to capitalize on the effects. We will address these concerns in the following chapters.

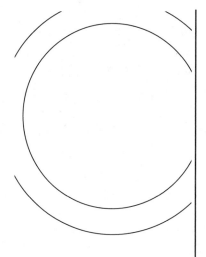

THREE

Energy Blockages

A healthy person is filled with a personal energy force that is vibrant, dynamic, and constantly interacting with energies of the world.
~ Colleen Deatsman

Through the activities in the last chapter, you have been able to experience directly how your personal energy flows and moves, sparkles and swirls through an organized field of life and vitality. You have probably felt, and perhaps been able to see, the wheels and layers of your energy field as they spin, sending rivers of flowing energy throughout your systems to bathe you in a sea of your own life force. No doubt you have felt the power of this energy flow and have benefited from the energizing results. Even so, you may at times continue to struggle with periods of low energy or fatigue. This could be a symptom of energy blockages or leakages. This chapter will address the concerns of energy blockages, while chapter four will address the concerns of energy leakages.

WHAT ARE ENERGY BLOCKAGES?

Our energy field is dynamic, meaning that it is in its healthiest state when it is in constant motion. Should this energy flow become walled off, dammed up, or tied up in knots, we would find ourselves experiencing energy flow blockages. Energy blockages are obstructions in the energy body that block the free flow of personal life-force energy. Low energy, fatigue, illness, disease, pain, and chronic emotional discomfort are some of the physical manifestations of energy that is congested or no longer moving. This stagnant, blocked, or stuck area impedes the natural flow of life-force energy through the body, thus reducing the amount of energy available for use. This can happen, and be rectified, in a multitude of ways. We will explore the causes of blockages first, and then learn how to release them through energy movement activities that will revitalize and energize you.

The most common way that we inadvertently create energy blockages is by "building energetic walls" to keep other people and the world at bay. We do this because we feel that the world is unsafe. We live in fear of many things: failure, success, personal attack, and intimacy—anything that comes too close or feels like a threat to our body, mind, emotions, and who we think we are. We worry about all the possible "what ifs," and this festers in our mind, causing more fear and energy consumption. Indeed, there are very few people on this planet who have transcended fear and feel perfectly safe twenty-four hours a day, seven days a week. So we build walls to help us feel safe. This is a natural and generally unconscious way that we deal with deep and serious problems in our lives and in our world. Fear is a powerful emotion that can be an impediment to energy flow if we don't continually work on it. For many people, this problem grows over time due to life's struggles, and the energetic wall becomes thickened and fortified to the point that the exchange of even healthy energy is cut off.

The world may or may not be safe, depending upon one's perspective and lot in life, but the reality is that this is our world and we need to live in it in the healthiest way possible. When we live in fear, we live in a self-imposed prison of insecurity. Cutting ourselves off from others, the world, and our feelings only intensifies the problem and we set up more and more false barricades. A common alternate response if we don't barricade ourselves away from the world is that we cling to anything that gives us a feeling of safety and security, even if it is not healthy. This often happens in relationships where people stay together only for security, familiarity, and out of the fear of being alone. In these instances we inadvertently develop behaviors that are controlling or clingy, needing to hang on tightly to people and objects in our lives. These feelings create deadly tension and anxiety in the body that manifest as blockages in the energy field. To release blockages caused by fear, we need to be able to identify and release our fears in addition to increasing our energy flow. I strongly encourage you to explore and release your fears as you practice the activities in this chapter that will help you gradually remove your walls energetically.

One of the main reasons that we feel so unsafe in our world is that most of us are not taught effective ways to protect ourselves on an energetic level. As we learned in chapter two, we are born with a powerful natural system for interaction with the outside world that screens incoming and outgoing energy. If it is healthy, our energy field is a powerhouse of safety and protection, and we know how to use it to our best advantage. The problem is that many of us know very little about our energy field and how to stimulate it to protect us. In addition, many of us have weak or torn energy fields from stress, everyday struggles, wounding, or traumas that lead to energy drain and overload, which in turn leads to more wall building and disease. An effective way to stop this process is to heal and fortify our energy field. The activities in this chapter and the next are designed to do just that by energizing your energy field and fortifying your energy boundaries. As you stimulate your energy field to strengthen and heal, it will effectively protect you, and you will feel comfortable dismantling the walls that are no longer needed.

"Walling up" is one response to the struggles that we face in life. Equally as detrimental to our energy flow are the dammed up and "tied up in knots" responses. These are typically caused by built-up stress, and storing issues and emotions in our body and energy field. When we don't relax and alleviate stress or we don't address and process our issues and the emotions associated with them, we carry them around energetically. As we repress these piggyback energies, they use up more and more of our personal energy and eventually manifest as debilitating symptoms.

A typical example is that many of us have achy necks or shoulders during times of stress. This is a place many of us hold tension, causing us to feel as if we are "carrying the weight of the world upon our shoulders." It is no wonder that several of the diagnostic trigger points of fibromyalgia are found here. We store a lot of emotion in our body, mind, and energy field as we live our lives. Therefore, it is imperative that we learn how to move energy through our energy field to continually release blockages before they manifest into full-blown energy loss, fatigue, or illness. Just taking a few minutes periodically during the day to relax, release tension, and activate energy flow will go a long way in energizing yourself and reestablishing vitality.

Many of our blockages form because we do not release stress regularly or take good care of ourselves. Self-love, honor, and nurturance are key components to combating stress. Our inner wisdom tells us that we need to love and honor ourselves, but our external programming has often taught us differently. In our world of doing, producing, and taking care of others, we have not learned the therapeutic importance of taking care of ourselves. In order to accomplish this, we must reprogram ourselves through our personal choices. We must choose a path of self-nurturance and give to ourselves, even if it feels uncomfortable at first. By practicing ongoing self-care for our soul, body, emotions, and mind, we keep an even flow of energy moving through our body and energy field. Harmony and balance then become our normal state of being.

Show yourself love and nurturance wherever, whenever, and however you can. Pamper yourself often and thoroughly. Nourish yourself with your own attention. It can be as simple as taking a hot bath, wrapping up in a fluffy comforter, or savoring a delicious cup of soothing tea. It could be saying nice things to yourself as you drive to work or to pick up the kids, giving yourself time to do the energy-moving activities in this book, or perhaps just resting when you need to. It might be as simple as giving yourself the gift of time to just *be*, a few moments of not doing anything. It's amazing how energizing it can be to watch the clouds roll by or the birds play in the birdbath. Perfection is a myth, and self-denial in the pursuit of such a myth is folly. Be good to yourself, and allow yourself to play. Do something, anything, that brings you pleasure. All work and no play is unbalanced and harmful. Allow the child inside of you to be free. Unleash your true self. Break the shackles that bind you. Enjoy! Life is not a competitive sporting event.

An important component to self-care and liberating dammed or tied-up energy blockages is to feel, nurture, and explore your emotions and feelings. Emotions and feelings are precious gifts that many of us neglect and avoid. The very word *emotion* correctly implies that these are the forces that get us moving. Emotions crystallize our resolve, stimulate our energy, and move us to action, and are therefore the essence of all dynamism in our lives. Without them, we would be hollow and stagnant, and we wouldn't care what happens to ourselves or to others. Emotions and feelings keep us engaged with life and help us experience humanity. But because we don't know how to effectively feel, understand, and honor our emotions and feelings, we give them power over us. We become afraid that they may overwhelm us or cause us discomfort and pain, so we ignore them, hoping that they will go away. But they don't go away. They go deeper inside and well up in our energy field and in the cells of our body. This emotional repression can begin to dam up the flow of energy or tie up the energy in knots as our circular thoughts go around and around in our head.

Symptoms such as low energy, fatigue, illness, pain, relentless mind chatter, and emotional distress may seem negative, but they are actually assets that signal distress from your energy field. By becoming quiet and experiencing your emotions and feelings, you can discern the internal messages that can guide you toward harmony and balance. Oftentimes, just allowing yourself to feel what you are feeling releases the energy blockage. Other times, you may need to stimulate your energy flow to dissolve the blockage. Either way, when you regularly honor your emotions and feelings, they act as a catalyst for a psychological and energetic revolution that frees you from energetic blockages and mental and emotional discord. By using techniques of discovery and release, such as the following activities, you can stimulate your mind and soul to investigate the true meanings of your emotions and feelings. This practice opens your awareness, and instead of avoiding emotions and feelings or being ruled by them, you can harness their messages for personal growth and their power for energizing. This allows you to dissolve the blockages and function in new and different ways that free you from your old energy-depleting patterns. It is by honoring the presence, messages, origins, and direction of your emotions and feelings that you keep your energy flowing, allowing you to fully experience life.

It is important that, as you honor and nurture your emotions and feelings, you avoid the trap of unhealthy excess. Dwelling too long on your emotions, or getting sucked into the adrenaline rush of powerful emotions, can turn into a huge energy drain. Holding on to feelings and emotions for too long can also cause you to inadvertently hold on to drama and trauma, causing destructive stress that exacerbates the blockages. Honor and acknowledge whatever you are feeling, and then employ your skills of awareness to discern the message. Open your energy channels and release the held emotions and energy using the activities that follow. Dip in for short periods of time, and then stand back and let go of the process for a while. Check in with yourself often to be sure that your process is not consuming you. If you find that you are feeling preoccupied and unavailable (to participate in your daily life), run more energy through your body and energy field until you feel lighter. When you resume your process you will have more energy, power, and clarity.

Another way that our energy field becomes blocked or restricted is from intrusions. Intrusions are energetic manifestations of thoughts, words, or emotions that are lodged in our energy field, causing wounding and energy blockage. Intrusions come from two places, one external and the other internal. External intrusions are sent by others either intentionally or unintentionally. Harsh words, verbal and physical confrontations, angry thoughts, and potent emotions are a few examples of where external intrusions originate. Internal intrusions come from ourselves in similar forms and are often described as self-destructive thoughts, feelings, and behaviors. These include those degrading things we do to ourselves like standing in front of the mirror saying, "Wow, you are fat" (or "ugly" or "stupid"). This may seem minor, but strong words propelled by potent emotions jab into our energy field and obstruct our energy flow. Likewise, excesses such as food, alcohol, laziness, compulsiveness, and doing too much cloud our energy flow. The list of intrusion possibilities is endless, making it vitally important that we protect ourselves from external and internal attacks by removing intrusions that already exist, strengthening our energy flow, and rectifying our self-sabotaging thoughts, words, emotions, and behaviors.

Now that we have identified the many ways that blockages form, it is time to learn and practice the self-exploration and energy movement exercises that will help you achieve vibrant energy flow. You are in charge of your own energy, and through choice, intention, and awareness, you can free yourself from the bondage of energy flow obstruction. When you are consciously awake and aware, no one knows you as well as you do. The most powerful way to explore your blockages is to allow your own energy, emotions, and body to speak directly to you. Once you have received all pertinent information, release the blockages by using the activities that follow.

Why Would I Want to Remove Energy Blockages?

We live in a world where most of us do not feel energized, powerful, or safe, even those of us who live in free countries far away from war zones. Stress, tension, everyday obligations, pressures, and interactions with others and our world leave us feeling vulnerable and uneasy. Many days we feel battle weary, as if we are terminally engaged in some kind of invisible conflict. This kind of stress gets under our skin, impacts our life-force, and depletes our energy. The unfortunate reality is that we will always have stress, tension, obligations, pressures, and interactions. It is the nature of our human life. The good news is the more we work to release blockages, stimulate our energy flow, and build healthy energetic boundaries, the more powerful we will feel and the more energy we will have to boldly face life's challenges. This in turn will prevent further blockages. With dynamic, free-flowing energy and power, we will have infinite energy to feel great and live life fully!

How to Remove Energy Blockages

Removing energy blockages can best be accomplished by employing the power of your own energy and mind. Using your intention, stimulate your personal energies to gather at the sites of the blockages. Use all of your senses to focus on the flow of your energy, and notice it begin to cut through and disintegrate those blockages. As the blockages dissolve, the residual energy is washed away in the flow of your energy rivers and transmutes into healthy, life-giving energy. If you could look inside yourself and see what is happening, it would look similar to drain cleaner eating through a clog in the pipes and then being washed away by the flow of the water. The following activities will guide you through this process.

The guided journey will help your mind and body relax as you are gently guided into an altered state of consciousness. While in this state you will access your internal wisdom and your internal healer and begin to see, sense, feel, and heal any blockages in your body and energy field. This is followed by a meditation and several energy blockage removal exercises. All of these activities utilize the skills of mental focus, attention, awareness, mindfulness, visualization, and intention. Some of the exercises also include body movement.

GUIDED JOURNEY

Activate Your Internal Wisdom and Healer

It is sometimes difficult to ascertain the exact origin of the energy blockage problem that you are dealing with. By becoming relaxed and aware, you can connect with your inner wisdom to learn about the locations, causes, and symptoms that you are experiencing. Once you become aware of the causes of your discomfort, you can connect with your inner healer to correct these imbalances and restore natural health and vitality. These aspects, your inner healer and your inner wisdom, are powerful aspects of yourself that form the backbone of your energizing practice. Your inner healer is the aspect of yourself that activates your natural inner healing abilities. Your inner wisdom is the aspect of yourself that is your inner guide, your intuition, and your inner knowing. Now sit back, take in a deep breath, and relax as you journey into the depths of your soul to meet and activate these two powerful internal allies.

Go to your soft space where you will be undisturbed, darken the room, and turn off all phones. Play any soothing, relaxing music that you enjoy. Sit or lie down where you will feel warm and comfortable, safe and protected. Take a moment to quiet yourself and allow yourself to become deeply relaxed using the Universal Induction.

As you continue to relax, send your awareness around and through the inside of yourself, and notice what is happening in your body and energy field. Allow yourself to feel what your body feels. Pay attention to each organ and each system, noticing its color, energy, and pulsating rhythm. Now allow yourself to feel what your energy field feels. Pay attention to each chakra and layer, noticing its color, energy, and pulsating rhythm. See, sense, and feel how your body and energy field work together doing a beautiful rhythmic dance of life, and enjoy this for a few moments. (long pause)

When you are ready, send the inquiring part of your mind into your body and energy field and ask them to "talk" to you and listen, really listen. "Hear" and feel what is being communicated. Carry on a conversation with each layer of your energy field, each individual chakra, and each cell, organ, and system of your body, and ask them to communicate with you. (long pause)

Through awareness and communication with your body and energy field, allow yourself to see, sense, and feel if you have any energy imbalances, blockages, or areas where your energy flow is sluggish. If you do, give yourself permission to feel whatever you are feeling and explore the issues surrounding your imbalanced, blocked, or weak energy flow. Listen to your inner wisdom. What is the blockage or imbalance? Where does it come from? Why is it there? Notice if there is a color associated with the blockage. If so, what is the significance of this color? Is it related to a chakra or a specific layer of your energy field? Is it related to a certain organ or system of your body? Notice if there is a feeling associated with the blockage. What significance does this feeling have for you? What else do you need to know about this? What can be done to remove this blockage? (long pause)

Send your awareness deeper into your inner wisdom now by moving into the area of the blockage. Become familiar and intimate with this area. Spend some time there, become friends, and feel what it's like there. Be aware of anything that you notice. Be open, feel, and listen with your inner knowing. Ask why the blockage happened in this area, and if it could talk to you, what would it tell you? Allow words and feelings to bubble forth into your conscious mind. Let this area know that you hear what it is telling you, and that you will honor its requests to the best of your abilities. (long pause)

Send the area love and attention, and begin the process of healing the blockage by gathering the power of your energy flow to the area. See, sense, and feel the powerhouse of your flowing energy come pouring into the area. You may feel warmth and tingling, and a sense of potency.

These feelings continue to increase in intensity as the energy congregates and a sense of pressure builds. With more and more energy arriving, the tension rises and begins to churn with excitement. The excited energy now swirls and pushes forward into the blockage. See, sense, and feel the healing power of your energy dissolving, disintegrating, and flushing away the blockage. Feel the change in your body and energy field. Be aware of how good you feel when your energy is flowing freely and strongly. Send your energy field love and gratitude for working hard to keep you healthy. Feel the nurturing effects of your love and affection being received and absorbed by your energy field. Allow yourself to see and feel the healing effects right now, as they are happening within you. Your inner healer is healing your energy field. See it and feel it happening. (long pause)

Continue to listen to the messages and wisdom of your body and energy field, and ask if there are any more imbalances or blockages that need to be healed and released. If so, repeat the steps above as many times as needed until the energy flowing through your entire body and energy field is free and unrestricted. Be aware of anything that you notice. Be open. Sense and listen with your inner knowing.

Once you have cleared all the blockages, your inner healer will continue restoring the natural harmony and balance in your body, mind, emotions, soul, energy field, and energy boundaries that create dynamic energy. See, sense, and feel this happening right now, and allow the images and feelings to swim around in your mind. Imagine every atom of your entire being saturated in a sea of soft, rainbow, swirling energy. Your muscles, bones, organs, systems, cells, chakras, and layers drink in the dynamic energy until you overflow with vitality, super energy, health, harmony, and balance. Feel the energy! Feel the power! (long pause)

Hold the images and your sensations for as long as you have time for, and when you are ready to return, count back from twenty-one to one, slowly open your eyes, and allow yourself time to shift. Be gentle with yourself, take in a deep breath, and notice how you feel.

Allow yourself to gently return to full ordinary consciousness. Take a few moments to just notice what you feel with all the senses of your body, your thoughts, and your emotions. You don't have to do anything with these feelings—just notice them. Become aware of what remains the same, and of any changes that you may sense. Write your thoughts and feelings in your journal, fully expressing yourself as deeply and openly as possible.

MEDITATION

Explore and Release Energy Blockages

Choose a place where you feel comfortable, perhaps in nature or in your soft space. Sit in quiet contemplation where you will not be disturbed. Open your mind and relax. Observe, notice, experience, and feel everything that you think and sense. Focus your attention on your body, and become aware of your energy field. Use all of your senses to experience your energy flowing in, through, and around you. Allow any distracting thoughts to drift away. Notice them and let them go.

Sit in quiet contemplation with the concept of energy blockage. Connect with your inner wisdom to gain insight on how and where you may be blocking energy. Are there places in your body and energy field where energy is blocked? If so, how? Is it dammed up? Knotted up? Walled off? Are there certain issues or stresses that are stored there that are causing the blockage of your energy? If so, thoroughly explore these. What can you do to remove the blockages now? Are there ways to reduce the external pressures that hold the blockage in place? Can you modify your life to include healthy practices for yourself that will reinstate and maintain a strong and balanced energy flow? If so, what?

Continue to sit quietly, and observe your energy for a while. See and feel, imagine and sense everything about your energy field, energy boundaries, and how and where the flow of your energy may be blocked or slug-

gish. *What do you notice? What do you think? What do you feel? What do you sense? Relax and allow yourself to sense and feel your life-force energy. Allow yourself to sense and feel the rhythm, pulse, and flow of your personal energy through your body and energy field. Notice your sensations.*

Now close your eyes and allow your inner wisdom to bubble forth. Relax, focus, and feel. Allow questions and answers to form in and out of your thoughts. Questions like: What does my energy feel like? What does my energy look like? What do the energy blockages feel like? What do the energy blockages look like? How strong are the blockages? Does this change from day to day? Hour to hour? Moment to moment? If so, what causes the change? Is my energy field affected by the energy of others? Are the blockages affected by the energy or interactions of others? If so, in what ways? Is this healthy? Do I need to change anything about this? Do I need to do anything in my daily life to prevent energy blockages? Do I need to do anything to strengthen and balance my energy flow? Do I need to know anything more about my energy? If so, what?

Stay in this place in contemplation for as long as you have time, asking your own questions of yourself. When you are ready, take in a deep breath and allow yourself a few moments to shift your awareness back to ordinary life and fully integrate back into your body.

BLOCKAGE REMOVAL EXERCISES

If your life seems overcast and dull and you are running low on energy, the wall-busting, dam-breaking, knot-disintegrating exercises that follow will free your energy and brighten your outlook. They can be performed anywhere at any time since you do not need to enter into an altered state of consciousness for them to be effective. Practice these exercises quickly whenever you are in need, or, if you have the time and are in an appropriate place for added relaxation and receptivity, you may choose to enter into an altered state of consciousness, as described in chapter one, before practicing these exercises.

Blockage Sieve

The first powerful blockage-clearing exercise utilizes your visualization powers to imagine a Blockage Sieve. When I first began teaching this exercise I guided students to visualize the sieve as a white sheet. Over the years I have expanded this exercise to include other images so people could choose an image that best suited their cleansing needs at the time. An example of how this exercise can be used comes from Betsy, a former client and student, who recently shared that she had been experiencing many energetic "arrows" lodging in her energy fields, so she used the white spirit sheet exercise to remove those "arrows" and purify her fields.

Using your imagination and all of your senses, see, sense, and feel yourself standing inside a huge metal sieve or on top of multiple layers of cheesecloth. Slowly and mindfully bring the sieve or cloth up through your body, raising it up way over your head as if you are sifting yourself through the holes in the mesh or the pores in the cloth. See, sense, and feel all of the darkness and congestion being pulled out of your body and energy field and remaining in the sieve or cloth as it passes through you. Release the sieve or cloth and its contents to the universe for transformation. See, sense, and feel yourself clear of walls, dams, and knots that once blocked your energy. See, sense, and feel yourself clear of any and all unwanted and unhealthy energies. Repeat three times or until totally clear.

Energy Field Sweeping

Another way to clear away unwanted or blocked energy is called Energy Field Sweeping. You can do this exercise standing or sitting down.

Take in a deep breath and relax for a moment. When you are ready, begin making sweeping motions with your hands over the surface of your body, brushing away any unwanted or accumulated energetic debris from your auric field. You can touch your body as you brush, or brush just above your body. Brush up and down and all around you. Brush over your hair and skin and clothes. Don't forget the top of your head and the bottom of your feet. If you are feeling stress and tension in your upper body, take extra time around your shoulders, neck, and head. Try this now for as long as you have time, and experiment with how it feels. If you are aware and able to feel your energy, it might feel tingly or like a gentle combing. You may also get a sensation similar to when you get an energetic chill down your spine, goosebumps, or when your hair raises. These are ways that you already sense energy. Sometimes this feels familiar and nurturing, like a cat bathing itself. It may also feel foreign or heavy if there is a lot of energy to move or this is a new experience for you. Even though this appears to be an external energy moving exercise, energy will also move deep within your body.

The Shake Off

Another effective and simple way to clear blockages and unwelcome energy is to literally shake off, like a dog shakes its coat, or to move around. This action stimulates stagnant energy to start moving. This is one of the many reasons that yoga and exercise are so beneficial. By taking just a few moments out of your day to stand up and move around or to shake off, you can move energy that will help to clear blockages before they are allowed to form from becoming stagnant.

Try the following activity now. Stand up, shake off, and move around for a few moments. Notice what you sense and feel. Shake until your muscles loosen and relax and you feel tingly all over.

Fire Energy

It is not unusual for energy blockages or physical manifestations of any of our issues to be deeply imbedded and difficult to affect. When this becomes apparent, I recommend utilizing this exercise to transform.

Begin by writing a letter. This letter can take many different forms. One way is to write to yourself about the manifestation of the blockage. Another is to write the letter directly to the blockage, expressing your emotions to it. Yet another way is to write the letter to the other person involved if your manifestation involves another. If your blockage is being caused by a situation, write your letter to the situation. These letters should be no-holds-barred, blatant, honest expressions of your emotions, including sadness, frustration, anger, or hatred—whatever you are feeling, without regard for spelling, punctuation, or profanity. No one will read these letters. Once written, having explored all aspects, burn the letter. Watch and feel as the words go up in flames of transformation. Feel your mind and emotions fully release the situation into the universe. Bury the ashes in the earth or flush them down the drain. Notice how your feel.

After a few moments, take in a deep breath, relax, and sit with the blockage you wrote about. Feel it, be with it, and listen to the messages that it brought to you. Then ignite the Energy of Fire in your own body through the inner flame of your life-force that resides in your solar plexus. Visualize and feel your inner flame. Nurture the flame and cause it to grow with your intention. Feel the heat in your center. Expand the flame into the affected areas of your body, and allow it to burn through the congested energy. See the residual energy leave your body like puffs of smoke. When all the energy has been transformed, reduce the flame to fit inside of your center. Feel it glowing there, take in a deep breath, relax, and notice how you feel.

Rainbow Waterfall

The Rainbow Waterfall exercise is a powerful energy clearing exercise that utilizes intention and visualization to cleanse energetic blockages and congestion from your body and energy field. The Rainbow Waterfall exercise is included on the accompanying CD as it is written here.

Close your eyes, take in a deep breath, and relax. Allow your imagination to take you on a tropical vacation. See, feel, sense, and experience yourself standing or sitting in a warm, calm, shallow pool of crystal clear water in a beautiful tropical paradise. Exquisite gardens surround you. To your left and right, steep mountainsides climb toward the sky, covered in thick, lush, green vegetation. The air carries a hint of moisture, and the faint perfumed fragrance of orchids lingers around you.

From the top of the mountain, a warm, gentle waterfall, sparkling with droplets of rainbow prisms, cascades down onto, around, and into your body. The soft, colorful waterfall penetrates into your energy field and body, washing away any energy blockages or congestion as it flows down through you and into the pool. With each inhalation, feel and fully sense the energy of the rainbow waterfall flow in through the top of your head and glide down through your face, back of your head, neck, shoulders, arms, chest, upper back, torso, stomach, lower back, legs, knees, and ankles, moving out through the bottom of your feet into the pristine pool. The unwanted energy that caused the blockages and congestion washes out of your body and energy field into the clear pool, and flows away down a small, trickling stream. Breathe deeply, relax, and feel the warm, soothing energy of the waterfall cleanse and heal you. Take in another deep breath, and feel, sense, and experience the energizing colors.

On your next inhalation, feel and fully sense the energy of the rain-bow waterfall flowing in through the top of your head, gliding down through the inside of your body, sliding over the outside of your body, and flowing down through your energy field into the pristine pool. Breathe deeply, relax, and feel the warm, soothing energy cleanse and energize you. Continue standing or sitting in the energy flow of the rainbow waterfall for as long as you have time. When you are finished, take a deep breath and open your eyes, feeling cleansed and energy-filled.

This is very powerful to perform periodically throughout the day to keep yourself energetically clean, and is particularly effective any time that you are taking a "real" shower. The Rainbow Waterfall is a favorite of my students, and many report using it several times a day to clean away any energetic debris they may have picked up before it becomes congested in their energy field. Sally is one of many who describes her experience with the Rainbow Waterfall as an effective tool.

"For me, the Rainbow Waterfall is a nurturing trip back to my native Puerto Rico, where beautiful waterfalls pouring down from lush mountains are a common find. I love the feel of the energy gliding down through my body and energy field as I imagine that I am standing under my favorite one. I am an administrator in an inner city public school system, where backbiting and political maneuvering are as common as truancy and fighting among the students. There is a lot of psychic energy flying around there that I need to clear myself of regularly. The Rainbow Waterfall is a refreshing and peaceful way for me to stay healthy."

Internal Rainbow Fountain of Energy

The Internal Rainbow Fountain of Energy exercise is a dynamic exercise that efficiently removes blockages while stimulating your personal energy and fortifying your energetic boundaries. It entails consciously awakening your personal life-force energy and moving it through your body and energy field, creating a fountain of flowing energy. This exercise not only stimulates your personal energy and clears energy blockages, it also seals energy leakages and naturally provides a shield of energetic protection around you. It'll leave you feeling whole, centered, and energized.

Begin by standing with your feet hip distance apart, arms down at your sides. Close your eyes and take in a deep breath. Keep breathing deeply throughout the exercise, using the breath and your intention to open and move the energy. Allow yourself to relax; perhaps slip into alpha if you choose. Place your attention on the soles of your feet and the crown of your head. Take in a deep breath and notice how you feel. Do a mental scan of your body, noticing any places where there may be pain, tightness, or tension signaling a blockage. If you become aware of a blockage, don't do anything about it—just notice it. After a few moments, focus your consciousness on your foot chakras located in the arches of both feet. See and sense the chakras ignite with a soft brownish-maroon energy. See that brownish-maroon ball of energy grow and expand, becoming a radiant source of glowing, maroon light that begins to saturate all of the tissues in your body. See and feel this light soaking into your abdomen, chest, head, and out your arms, bathing organs, muscle, blood, and bone until your entire body becomes a great neon beacon of this light. After a few moments, allow that maroon energy to recede once again back to its home in your foot chakras, where it continues to glow and spin brightly. After a few moments, focus your consciousness on your root chakra located at the base of your torso where your legs meet your body. See and sense the chakra ignite with a deep, vibrant, red energy. See that red ball of energy grow and expand, becoming a radiant source of glowing, ruby-red light that begins to saturate all of the tissues in your body. See and feel this light soaking into your abdomen, chest, head, and out your arms, bathing organs, muscle, blood, and bone until your entire body becomes a great neon beacon of this light. After a few moments, allow that ruby energy to recede once again back to its home in your base chakra, where it continues to glow and spin brightly.

After a few moments, take in another deep breath, and focus your consciousness on your sacral chakra. See and sense it spinning and glowing with a bright orange light. As before, stir this energy and expand it throughout your body, saturating every cell with this orange, regenerative light. Once again, after a few moments, shrink the light back to its home in your second chakra, where it continues to spin and glow a brilliant orange.

Use this same technique for the brilliant sunshine-yellow energy of your solar plexus chakra, for the emerald-green of your heart chakra, for the gold in the palms of your hands, for the azure-blue of your throat chakra, for the deep indigo of your third-eye chakra, for the pale violet of your crown chakra, and for the crystalline translucence of your universal chakras. Each time, stimulate and spin the chakra energy wheel, using your intention and your breath to create the characteristic spectral light of each chakra. Take the time to permeate your entire being with each of the energies before moving on to the next.

When all chakras have been energized, continue to see and feel them spinning and glowing in each of their homes, washing and penetrating all of your tissues. On your next inhalation, draw this rainbow energy up from your feet, through your center, and out the top of your head like a fountain. As the energy exits your head, see and feel it as rainbow droplets that cascade out to the limits of your aura and down again to your feet. As these rainbow droplets mist through your auric field, see your aura cleansed and refreshed by the movement of this energy. Continue this until the limits of the luminous egg that is your energy field have been completely energized, and keep this rainbow fountain flowing as long as you need to by maintaining the focus of your attention on the energy movement. There is no need to shut down the circulating energies around and through you. When you are finished, take a deep breath and open your eyes, feeling cleansed and energy-filled. Energy in motion tends to stay in motion, so the benefits of this exercise continue long after you have finished it.

I imagine at this point that strongly flowing vibrant energy is giving you a new lease on life from practicing the energy connecting and blockage removal journeys and exercises in the past two chapters. I hope that you are making time in your busy life on a regular basis to refresh your energy supply and keep your energy moving. If you are, you are probably feeling some pretty powerful benefits. Keeping your energy stimulated and clear is essential to feeling energized. Sometimes, even when we are diligent in our energy connecting and moving practice, energy leakages overload or drain away our energy, limiting our ability to maintain high levels of energy. These concerns will be addressed in the following chapter.

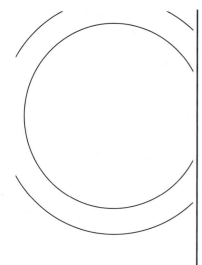

FOUR

Energy
Leakages

*A high-energy person
doesn't waste energy.
- Colleen Deatsman*

Tired of being tired? Want to become *fully* energized? If the natural vitality and sparkle of your personal energy have waned and you have cleared all your blockages, the problem may be weak energy boundaries that allow energy overload or draining. Revitalizing your energy is the first step. Prevention of energy loss is the second. This chapter will teach you how to do both efficiently and easily. The activities in this chapter will help you stop and prevent leakages by consciously activating and stimulating your personal energy field and intentionally fortifying your energetic boundaries. This will revitalize your energy and make more energy available for your own use. The goal in maintaining high energy levels is to use as much of your own energy for yourself as you possibly can. If you are leaking energy you will have less energy available to you.

Throughout this chapter we will explore the many different ways that energy can be lost, so that you will be able to recognize where you are leaking energy and make changes that will help you keep your energy for yourself. I believe in the philosophy that prevention is the best cure. Let's explore energy loss first and then learn ways to stop the leakages and revitalize your energy field.

WHAT IS ENERGY LEAKAGE?

One of the main sources of energy loss is a weak and leaky energetic boundary. An energetic boundary is a semipermeable boundary around your body formed by the layers and chakras of your energy field. It looks like a luminous egg. Your energetic egg extends out from your body around three feet or just beyond your outstretched arms. Many of us know this to be our personal space or personal bubble, and are uncomfortable if someone enters that space without permission. This energetic boundary protects our personal energy by providing an invisible shield that screens incoming and outgoing energy, keeping our energy field a closed, contained system. Without this boundary our energy field might extend to infinity instead of staying in and around our body, where we need it for vitality and protection. A healthy, luminous energy boundary is essential to having vibrant physical energy.

Our wonderful luminous egg is one of the instruments that we use to sense, feel, and interact with the luminous eggs of others and the environment. Our energy field automatically scans every vibration that comes near it or enters it and sends us messages in the forms of sensations, feelings, and knowings. We experience these messages daily and usually respond to them without realizing where they come from. For example, we sometimes instantly sense an attraction to someone we just met, or feel punched in the gut by someone's angry words. Perhaps you have experienced situations where you have been given a warning by your energy field, like driving on a busy interstate expressway and somehow knowing that the car you are about to pass is going to swing into your lane without looking, so you slow down, and then it does. In so many ways all throughout our lives our energy boundary is our silent defender, as long as it's working properly. If it's not working correctly, one of the first things we experience is loss of energy and fatigue.

Healthy energy boundaries are semiporous and semipermeable to allow for exchanges of energy. If our energetic boundary is too porous or becomes torn or leaky, we may struggle with a variety of issues depending on the severity and location of the weakness or leak, and which layers and chakras are affected. As you may recall from chapter two, the layers and chakras of the energy field correlate with specific quality of life concerns; for example, our root chakra is associated with our will to live and our heart chakra is associated with our ability to give and receive love, so we can see that if I had a boundary weakness or leak in the fourth layer of my energy field it would correlate with my heart chakra and I might struggle with issues related to love and relationships. I would also experience other nonspecific, generalized effects in my body, mind, emotions, and spirit, because I am losing precious personal energy.

Loss of energy, fatigue, confusion, and illness are top on the list of physical and mental maladies experienced when our energy field is leaking. Obviously, when too much of our personal energy is leaking away, there is less for us to use for ourselves. Emotionally and energetically many people feel depressed or anxious when too much energy is slipping away. When our energy boundaries aren't healthy, we are also more vulnerable to incoming energy from external sources and we become overly empathetic and highly sensitive. When this occurs we may have a tendency to absorb the feelings, problems, or pain of others. I call this the "sponge effect" because we inadvertently soak up unwanted energy like a sponge. In other instances we may take on the behaviors and patterns of another and can lose our authentic self when this happens. The reverse is also a possibility; we give ourselves away to another person, wanting that person to rescue us, battle our problems for us, do too much for us, or act as a grounding agent for us. Psychology calls this co-dependency, but it's more than a psychological or personality problem; it is also an energy imbalance, and the energetic component can be healed by fortifying or repairing our energy boundary.

Weak energy boundaries and leakages can also inadvertently lead to energy blockages. When our energetic boundaries become too thin or torn and we don't know how to correct this energetically, we set up artificial boundaries to help protect us and make us feel safe. Oftentimes, these artificial boundaries are thick walls that prevent any energy from going out or coming in, blocking even the natural flow of healthy energy. This can lead to profound fatigue as well as feelings like loneliness, separateness, and lack of love and connection. In these situations it is best to stop the energy leakages and fortify your energy boundaries first. Once your energy boundaries become healthy you will probably feel the walls slowly disintegrate, as they are no longer needed. However, if you still feel blocked, keep fortifying your energetic boundary and willfully dismantle the wall with the energy blockage exercises from chapter three.

If you feel that you are struggling with any of these or any other energetic boundary problems, help is just around the corner with the activities given later in this chapter.

• • •

Even with strong, healthy energetic boundaries, energy loss occurs for multitudes of reasons, and that is why awareness, revitalization, and prevention are so important. We must become consciously aware of what is draining us and where our energy is going, and then work to correct problem areas.

The demands of life, stress, and spending too much of our personal energy are major sources of energy drainage. We buzz around like busy little bees, living our lives without awareness of where our energy goes. We feel exhausted a lot of the time but don't know what to do about it because we were never taught anything about energy use, other than our parents reminding us to turn the lights off when we leave a room. A clairvoyant person or a good woodsman tracker sees the energy traces left behind. Everywhere we go we leave a little residual energy trace. To illustrate, during some of my energetic training we did an exercise where the students were to enter into an altered state of consciousness and go out on the property of the retreat center. We were instructed to walk around and find the teacher who would physically stay in the meeting room but project herself energetically out onto the grounds. Not only did the students find the energy of the teacher in specific places in her present adult form, but they also found her playing in specific places as a child. At first this was confusing, until our teacher recalled that this retreat center had been a summer camp that she had attended as a child. We were seeing the residual traces of her presence from many years ago.

So we can see that even in simple, ordinary situations we leave a little residual energy in our wake. In stressful situations we leave more energy. When we feel strong emotions, we emit a lot of energy. When we struggle and strain to survive, we lose energy. This is natural and not a detriment. The detriment comes when we lose too much energy and are not able to replenish it. When we deal with a constant barrage of stressors and responsibilities (even positive ones) we become drained. When this draining goes on for long periods of time without respite, we become physically exhausted. This pattern of exhaustion begins to weaken our energetic boundaries, leaving us vulnerable to more loss of energy.

As the losses compound, our life-force energy gradually diminishes and fatigue and low energy become common companions. We become tired and less powerful, and it feels like we are rushing in to fight another battle, still wounded from the last one. We are not as strong and fast as before, and this makes us vulnerable to more wounding.

This is how many illnesses and diseases take hold, and this is why many ailments are actually imbalances caused from energy and power loss. When we continually waste our personal energy without revitalizing our essential life-force, we keep re-exhausting and re-wounding ourselves, and we never get refilled with energy.

To break this pattern it is of primary importance that you be conscious and aware of where you are spending your energy. Look over your day, your activities, and your internal world of thoughts and emotions, noticing where you are spending your energy. Are you giving away too much energy to others, to work, or to certain situations? Are you draining your own energy by doing too much, thinking too much, feeling too much, or being self-indulgent? Take a few moments to assess your energy expenditures, and then ask yourself, "Is this really where I want to be spending my energy?" Allow yourself to be open and honest, and, please, don't be hard on yourself or judgmental.

Pay attention to your energy expenditures throughout the day. Become mindful about the things you do, the emotions you feel, and the thoughts you think. What you focus on, you give energy to. What you give energy to, you give life to. If you give energy to worry and negativity, you give life to those things, allowing them to thrive in your world and drain your energy. Likewise, if you focus on love and positive outcomes, you give life to those things, and they will reign in your world and keep your energy vital. It's important to realize how you choose to spend your energy is a decision that is up to you. You may not be able to change a situation, but you can change how you choose to respond to it. The next time you find yourself faced with a difficult or stressful situation, try focusing on prayer and a positive outcome instead of on the scary "what ifs." At the very least you have changed your response to one that is more energetically healthy for you.

Thoughts and emotions are energy spent. Check in with yourself periodically to see how much you are thinking and feeling, and become aware of how much mental and emotional energy you are spending. Pay particular attention to circular thoughts and feelings, those thoughts and feelings that go around and around in your head without resolution, as these are a huge energy drain. These may be indicators of unresolved difficult situations or traumas in your life that are draining you energetically. The cycle of repetitive thoughts and feelings is incredibly draining and fatiguing. When you catch yourself in this pattern you need to break the cycle by changing your thought pattern and replenishing your energy field and boundaries using the activities given later in this chapter.

With awareness, you can choose to change what you give energy to by watching your thoughts, prioritizing responsibilities, and honoring yourself with daily energizing disciplines instead of wasting energy on needless worries and negative thoughts. In this way, you can save and direct your energy toward enjoying and fully living life. I recommend that you print the precept "What you give energy to, you give life to," and hang it around the house and office to remind yourself daily of your choice to manifest the energy and life you want. Mine is superimposed on a tranquil mountain scene that also helps me connect with nature.

Often we are not aware of how much personal energy we willingly give to others. When family or friends ask for help, we willingly open our heart and soul, unconsciously transferring our personal energy to them. We are not aware that we are giving them our valuable life-force energy, nor are they aware that they are receiving it. Most people don't realize that we are not able to use another's energy for very long. The only truly valuable energy is our own or the universal life-force, so depleting oneself for the sake of others helps no one. It's wonderful to help others, but do so only in ways that can really help them, like teaching them to connect with their own energy. A perfect example of this was a situation that happened to me in my early days of working as a mental health counselor. I was unaware of personal energy at the time and didn't realize that I was handing out my energy to nearly every client I worked with. For many years, I had been compassionately helping people become awake, aware, alive, and to grow and heal. I did this by looking into them to find the source of their problem, energetically drawing it out to help them become aware and able to address it, and then inadvertently giving them access to my personal energy to use to correct the problem.

Over time, I began to experience the increasingly debilitating physical symptoms of chronic fatigue immune deficiency syndrome. Try as

I might, I could not determine what the causes of my problems were. Eventually, after exploring several different types of energetic body work in the attempt to heal my body, I discovered the nature of my problems. The great blessing and curse of my healing style was that when I "looked into" my clients, then "reached into" them, I also linked with them energetically and existed inside of their personal energy environment for varying periods of time. That was a necessary part of my therapeutic ability. What I failed to do was to completely disengage from my clients and refortify my energetic boundaries after my work was done. I was unwittingly keeping an energetic doorway open to my clients, through which I was being drained. In essence, I was taking on the energy body burdens of one hundred plus people over time; or, at the very least, I was having my personal energy wicked off by many of them. Because my original training as a therapist was from traditional academia, I had not received any training on ways to protect my energy body and completely break the connection with my clients. Once I determined what was going on, I developed and employed the protection techniques described later in this chapter. They will work equally well for you.

The reason I use this story to illustrate my point is to show how so many of us become susceptible to the effects of a weak energy boundary through compassionate giving. Even the most aware and gifted among us are susceptible to having their energy bled away if they do not maintain strong, healthy energy boundaries. If you are involved in a helping situation, you must remain self-protected and teach those around you how to manifest their own energy, perhaps by using the energy replenishing exercises we will explore soon, or by building on strengths they already possess. Be aware of what your energy is doing when you are trying to help someone. With focus and intent, consciously keep your personal energy to yourself. Often, those who come to us for help (except in the case of healing professionals) really don't want us to fix them— they just want us to listen. They don't want or need our energy—they just want our attention and understanding.

Conversely, there are those individuals who do want our energy. In my experience, they come in two categories. There are those who are wounded and go around sucking up the energy of others in an attempt to fill themselves with good vibrations; then there are those who bear strong hatred or jealousies and whose strong emotions knock life-force energy out of their perceived enemy. Both of these types can drain energy unknowingly or knowingly from their objects of focus. The power of the mind and emotion is incredible and reaches far beyond the awareness of the general public. We all have people in our lives who leave us feeling drained and powerless after spending time with them. We are usually not aware that they are knowingly or unknowingly sucking us dry of our vital life-force. For lack of a better term, they are energy vampires. Whether attempting to fill themselves with our healing energy or trying to destroy us with their malice toward us, the effect is the same energy drain that results in power loss. The first step in protecting our precious energy is awareness. We must protect our treasured commodity of energy by strengthening our energetic boundaries and keeping our personal energy active and vital through focus and intent. When we are filled with powerful energy we are protected and strong energetically.

Energy cord connections with others are a natural occurrence and are generally healthy. Energy cords are luminous cords or chains that form between people, pets, objects, and sometimes places during relationships and interactions. Energy cords look like glowing telephone wires or cable cords that run between us and others and act as energy conduits. We grow energy cords from our chakras and allow them to permeate our energy boundaries and energy field to provide a connection and a natural flow of energy give and take. The cords act as energetic conduits whereby the individuals send each other messages in the forms of thoughts, feelings, and emotions. This can be very healthy and is indeed how we energetically have intimate relationships. Energy cords are very apparent between mothers and children, and between lovers.

Energy cords can become a source of energy drain or overload when they become too strong, too thick, or when vinelike smaller cords wrap around a healthy cord. In these instances, too much energy is flowing through the cords and the individuals may be losing their autonomy. Energy cords can be become extremely dangerous when one person is doing most of the giving or taking and there is not a balanced exchange of energy. The person being drained or overloaded generally begins to lose touch with his or her authentic self, experiences extreme fatigue, and becomes too enmeshed in the life of the other person. Typically, when relationships end, energy cords are torn. This can be quite painful. Sometimes energy cords remain after a relationship is finished, leaving an unhealthy connection and possible energy drain or overload. In these detrimental situations you may need to cut or disconnect the energy cords you have with another so that you can move on in a healthy manner or regain your own energy and authentic self.

Now that we've discovered all the ways that we've lost energy and learned how to try to prevent future energy loss, let's get our energy rolling! Too much stress, draining, overloading, and leaking leads to a very tired and unhappy person. I am inviting you to give yourself permission to take care of yourself. I am inviting you to give yourself permission to feed yourself with all the nurturance and energy you can handle. I am inviting you to give yourself permission to be yourself and to love yourself. By awakening your own powerful energy systems, you can have all the energy you want!

Of course, we all experience stress, struggle, and life-draining challenges. Not all energy loss can be prevented, so you must learn how to fuel up again. If you are a person who burns a lot of energy, then you need to fuel up regularly and powerfully throughout the day. Unfortunately, most of us are never taught how to access this kind of energy nourishment, so we struggle along low on energy or only partially refueling on the little things we do for ourselves. The following activities not only help replenish with energy that heals, they also build protection from energy loss. When you are power-filled, you are strong, vibrant, and powerful. From this place of power, when faced with life challenges, you will be better suited to handle them. Your connection to your own life-force energy will give you the internal strength to handle the outside struggles. If you perform the following exercises at least once a day (more if you can), you will be doing yourself a great refueling favor!

Why Would I Want to Stop Energy Leakages?

We are likely to always have positive, healthy interactions with others and our world, and also negative, threatening ones. We will have our idiosyncrasies, unhealthy behaviors, and lessons to learn that will come in the form of challenges. The good news is that the more we work to build healthy energetic boundaries, the less we will feel victimized by life and the less reactionary we will be when life's challenges come knocking on our boundary. This in turn will prevent further leakages. Not only that, but the stronger and healthier our energy field, the more energy we will have to meet these challenges. And as we meet our challenges gracefully and energetically we will have plenty of energy left over.

How to Seal Energy Leakages

There are many effective ways to seal energy leakages. It can be as simple as paying attention to and becoming aware of what is happening with your energy and then mentally employing your will to keep your energy with you. This requires focus and intention. You may find that through your personal assessment you need to change some of your behaviors or perceptions to keep your energy closer to home. If you are having problems with relationships you may be interested in the energy cord cutting and energy boundary fortification exercises. The following guided journey will help your mind and body relax as you are gently guided into an altered state of consciousness. While in this state you will access your internal wisdom and your internal healer and begin to see, sense, feel, and heal any leakages in your energy field. This is followed by a meditation and several energy fortification exercises. All of these activities utilize the skills of mental focus, attention, awareness, mindfulness, visualization, and intention. Some of the exercises also include body movement.

GUIDED JOURNEY

Seal Off Energy Leakages Using Your Internal Wisdom and Healer

Similar to blockages, it is sometimes difficult to ascertain the exact origin of the energy leakage problem that you are dealing with. By becoming relaxed and aware, you can connect with your inner wisdom to learn about the locations, causes, and symptoms that you are experiencing. Once you become aware of the causes of your energy loss, you can then connect with your inner healer to correct these imbalances and restore natural health and vitality. Now get comfortable, take in a deep breath, and relax as you journey into the depths of your soul to activate these two powerful internal allies.

Go to your soft space where you will not be disturbed, darken the room, and turn off all phones. Play any soothing, relaxing music that you enjoy. Sit or lie down where you will feel warm and comfortable, safe and protected. Take a moment to quiet yourself, and allow yourself to become deeply relaxed using the Universal Induction.

As you continue to relax, allow yourself to see, sense, and feel the natural flow and rhythm of your personal energy surrounding your body. Become aware of your whole energy field for a few moments. When you are ready, send the inquiring part of your mind into your energy field and ask it to "talk" to you and to listen, really listen. "Hear" and feel what is being communicated. Allow yourself to feel what your energy field feels. Carry on a conversation with your energy boundaries, each layer of your energy field, and each individual chakra, and ask them to communicate with you.

As you continue to communicate with your energy field, allow yourself to see, sense, and feel any energy leakages. If you do, give yourself permission to feel whatever you are feeling and explore the issues surrounding your energy loss. Listen to your inner wisdom. What is the leakage? Where does the leakage come from? Why is the leakage there? Notice if there is a color associated with the leakage. If so, what is the significance of this color? Is it related to a chakra or a specific layer of your energy field? Notice if there is a feeling associated with the leakage. What significance does this feeling have for you? What else do you need to know about this? What can be done to heal this leakage?

Send your awareness deeper into your inner wisdom now by moving into the area of the leakage. Become familiar and intimate with this area. Spend some time there, become friends, and feel what it's like there. Be aware of anything that you notice. Be open. Feel and listen with your inner knowing. Ask why the leakage happened in this area and, if it could talk to you, what would it tell you? Allow words and feelings to bubble forth into your conscious mind.

Send the area love and attention, and begin the process of healing the leakage by gathering the power of your energy flow to the area. See, sense, and feel the powerhouse of your flowing energy pouring into the area. You may feel warmth and tingling, and a sense of potency. These feelings continue to increase in intensity as the energy congregates and power builds. With more and more energy arriving, the tension rises and begins to churn with excitement. The excited swirling energy flows forward into the leakage and unites with the healthy energy field on all sides surrounding the leakage. It looks like the energy flowing into the leakage holds hands with the atoms around the leakage, keeping the new energy from being sprayed away until the hole is completely sealed and the energy field returns to its fully intact state. See, sense, and feel the healing power of your energy building, strengthening, and fortifying the area where the leakage once drained away or overloaded your energy. Feel the change in your body and energy field. Be aware of how good you feel when your energy is flowing freely, safely held near your body with strong energy boundaries. Send your energy field love and gratitude for working hard to keep you healthy. Feel the nurturing effects of your love and affection being received and absorbed by your energy field. Allow yourself to see and feel the healing effects right now, as they are happening within you. Your inner healer is healing your energy field. See it and feel it happening.

Continue to listen to the messages and wisdom of your body and energy field, and ask if there are any more leakages that need to be healed and released. If so, repeat the steps above as many times as needed until the energy flowing through your entire body and energy field is held safely within your energy boundaries. Be aware of anything that you notice. Be open, sense, and listen with your inner knowing.

Once you have sealed all the leakages, take in a deep breath and relax. Your inner healer will continue restoring the natural harmony and balance in your body, mind, emotions, energy field, and soul that create dynamic energy. See, sense, and feel this happening right now, and allow the images and feelings to swim around in your mind.

See, sense, and feel your energy field within and around your body. Beginning at the bottom of your feet, use all of your senses to experience each chakra spinning in all its glorious color. Take in a deep breath, and spend a few moments circulating the energy of each chakra. Slowly move your energy awareness up your body from your foot chakras to your root, sacral, solar plexus, heart, hands, throat, third eye, and crown chakras. Feel the energy spiraling around your body throughout your entire energy field, reaching out to your protective energy boundary. See, sense, and feel your energy boundary as a strong, healthy membrane of living, dynamic energy. Thicken and fortify the membrane if you need to, and send it love and gratitude for working hard to protect you. Within the membrane, see, sense, and feel your whole energy field and body saturated by vibrant rainbow swirling energy with a spiraling staircase of multicolored energy wrapped around your spine. Feel yourself enveloped in a vortex of colors and energy vibrations that infuses your entire being with love and power. Imagine every atom of your energy field teeming with dynamic power and energy. Vitality, super energy, health, harmony, and balance have once again been restored. Feel the energy! Feel the power!

Hold the images and your intention for as long as you have time, and when you are ready to return, count back from twenty-one to one, slowly open your eyes, and allow yourself time to shift. Be gentle with yourself, take in a deep breath, and notice how you feel.

Allow yourself to gently return to full ordinary consciousness. Take a few moments to notice what you feel with all the senses of your body, your thoughts, and your emotions. You don't have to do anything with these feelings—just notice them. Become aware of what remains the same, and of any changes that you may sense. Write your thoughts and feelings in your journal, fully expressing yourself as deeply and openly as possible.

MEDITATION

Sense and Close Energy Leakages

Choose a place where you feel comfortable, perhaps in nature or in your soft space. Sit in quiet contemplation where you will not be disturbed. Open your mind and relax. Observe, notice, experience, and feel everything that you think and sense. Focus your attention on your body, and becoming aware of your energy field. Use all of your senses to experience your energy flowing in, throughout, and around you. Allow any distracting thoughts to drift away. Notice them and let them go.

Sit in quiet contemplation with the concept of energy loss. Connect with your inner wisdom to gain insight into how and where you may be leaking energy. Are there places, situations, or people in your life that drain your energy? If so, thoroughly explore these. Are there ways to limit the amount of energy spent? Can you modify your energy expenditures to include healthy practices for yourself that will replenish, rather than deplete, your energy reserves?

Continue to sit quietly, and observe your own energy for a while. See and feel, or imagine and feel, everything about your energy field, energy boundaries, and how and where you spend your energy. What do you notice? What do you think? What do you feel? What do you sense? Relax and allow yourself to sense and feel your personal life-force energy. Allow yourself to sense and feel other energies around you, and notice how your energy interacts with other energies. Notice your sensations.

Now close your eyes and allow your inner wisdom to bubble forth. Relax, focus, and feel. Allow questions and answers to form in and out of your thoughts. Questions like: What does my energy feel like? How strong is my energy boundary? Does my energy field change from day to day? Hour to hour? Moment to moment? If so, what causes the change? Is my energy field affected by the energy of others? Of places? If so, in what ways? Is this healthy? Do I need to change anything about this? Do I need to do anything to strengthen my energy field? Do I need to do anything to strengthen my energy boundaries? Do I need to know anything more about how I spend my energy? If so, what?

Stay in this place in contemplation for as long as you have time, asking your own questions of yourself. When you are ready, take in a deep breath and allow yourself a few moments to shift your awareness back to ordinary life and fully integrate back into your body.

EXERCISES TO SEAL ENERGY LEAKAGES

The following energy leakage exercises can be performed anywhere at any time since you do not need to enter into an altered state of consciousness for them to be effective. They are superb energizers, efficient leakage stoppers, and potent fortifiers of energy boundaries. These exercises can be performed quickly whenever you are in need. For added relaxation and receptivity, if you have the time and are in an appropriate place, you may choose to enter into an altered state of consciousness, as described in chapter one, before performing these exercises.

Cord Cutting and Healing

Energy cord connections are generally healthy. Occasionally, these connections can become unhealthy and begin to drain or overload our energy field. The Cord Cutting and Healing exercise effectively disconnects any unhealthy connections or attachments and helps you to energetically heal from these without energetic scarring.

Relax and take in a deep breath. Close your eyes and visualize an empty screen. Place yourself on the left and the other person on the right. Imagine that you are separated by the symbol of infinity, which looks like a sideways figure eight. Allow this picture to fully form in your mind. Begin to see or feel any energetic cords that stretch between the two of you across the symbol. Take as much time as you need to really experience the cords. When you are ready, imagine a pair of golden scissors, and cut these energetic cords with the scissors. Feel and see that they are cut solidly. You may be guided to do additional steps, such as cauterizing the cords or lowering a solid wall between the two of you. See, sense, and feel the completeness of the cord cutting and tell yourself that "it is done." This exercise does not end your relationship with the other person, but brings it into balance by cutting the co-dependent, dependent, and karmic ties. This allows both of you to be independent and your relationship to be free and healthy.

Allow yourself a few moments to be aware of anything that you are experiencing. When you are ready, use all of your senses to see, sense, and feel your own nurturing personal energies gathering around the chakra areas associated with the places where you cut the cords. Feel the power of your own energy lovingly wrap around these areas and sink deep into your chakras and body. Relax and allow the energy to heal you. Take your time and really feel the healing as it happens. The deeper you take the healing, the more permanent and healthy your cord cutting experience will be, so relax and allow the healing to deepen within you for as long as you have time.

Please note that occasionally energy cords are strong ties that may return if permanent sealing measures were not taken, so repeating this exercise is recommended if symptoms persist.

Recently, my friend and student Fawn shared her powerful cord cutting experience with me and has graciously agreed to allow me to share it with you. She explains, "My divorce was extremely difficult. My husband had been having an affair with a younger woman and had gotten her pregnant. We had a two-year-old daughter, and I worked full time to support us. It was like swimming through mud every day. I was so depressed I functioned like a robot, getting the basic daily requirements over with and sleeping the rest of the time. It was a dramatic unfolding of events that left me bitter and physically ill.

"At one point, I was hospitalized after having surgery on both my appendix and a burst ovarian cyst. I had two car accidents—one a very serious close call. I ate unforgiveness for breakfast and anxiety for dinner. I had a recurring nightmare of a vampire who chased me everywhere until he caught me in my bedroom, held me down, and sucked away my life's blood. With no one to help me, I awoke in a cold sweat, feeling as if I were going to die. Instead of fighting against this, I went along with what was occurring inside of me. The letting go was a huge breakthrough because I was so very angry and sad. Yet from a spiritual level I pondered about what energy could cancel all this negativity out. I began to toy with the idea of visualizing something opposite of the bitter arrows of low, angry energy being sent to me from my husband and his girlfriend. In a moment of panic I prayed to the Light I felt as God. I asked for assistance in my visualization to send love and find detachment. As I prayed, the Light became strong and very, very bright. I was not alone, and the presence in my room was intense. I was shown a cord between myself and them—actually, two cords, one for each person connected to me. I was given ammunition and proceeded to explode our thick connection at first with dynamite, then with an ax, and finally with a giant knife to cut the frayed strings away. I sent the cord ends back to each person and sealed them off with red hearts full of love and forgiveness. I kept repeating over and over, 'I forgive you, I forgive me, I forgive us,' until my heart, mind, and soul actually *felt* the truth of the mantra. The Light grew even brighter, and I was showered with strength and joy. I felt healed and relieved!

"With the act of cord cutting and forgiving, I had completed our karmic dance once and for all. That drama was forever *over*, and I was elated! For the first time in months I slept well, and the next day when my husband returned to see our daughter my energy remained calm and thankful. He acted the same—emotionally distant and outwardly angry. I felt peace and calm. He began the usual recital of words that normally would start a fight, but I was 'over it.' Suddenly in the midst of his anger, I blurted out, 'I forgive you, I forgive me, I forgive us!' and proceeded to tell him I was moving forward with no hard feelings. I'll never forget his shocked face! Several suspicious days later I finally saw a change of behavior from both of them.

"Emotional relief began the night of the cord cutting. I'd transformed pain and fear into joy and thankfulness with this visualization. The effect was lasting and real. It was a miracle!"

Swirling Rainbow Cocoon

A powerful leakage sealer, boundary strengthener, and overall energizer, the Swirling Rainbow Cocoon exercise is highly recommended as a powerful healing tool.

Take a moment to relax, breathe deeply, and close your eyes. Use the power of your imagination to see yourself completely enveloped in a spiral of swirling rainbow energy. Focus on the soles of your feet and begin seeing, sensing, and feeling the rainbow colored energy swirl all the way up and down, inside and outside of your body and energy field. This swirling, healing, nurturing energy completely wraps you in a cocoon of infinite energy and power that fortifies your boundaries. See all of your energy leakages being sealed by this force, and feel yourself filled with energy. Experience this exercise for as long as you have time. When you are ready, open your eyes and return to your daily activities, maintaining the power of your rainbow cocoon.

Energy Protection Shields

Some people also find benefit from setting up Energy Protection Shields, whereby they encircle themselves in white light, a cobalt-blue egg, a pink circle of love, a swirling spiral of rainbow colors, a circle of roses, or a circle of mirrors. I've heard of many variations, and all are effective given one constant: that the person setting them up does so with disciplined focus using all of his or her senses to bring the shields to life. Randomly thinking you are protected is far different from consciously feeling the tangible energy surrounding you. To accomplish the desired degree of protection, you must go beyond just thinking it; you must focus your mind and experience it with your senses to manifest it with power.

The Circle of Mirrors Protection Shield

This is a powerful energy boundary protecting exercise.

Begin by taking in a deep breath, then exhale and let yourself relax, releasing any stresses or tensions that you may be feeling. Take in a few more deep, full breaths, and focus your mind on creating your energy shield. Visualize and tangibly feel yourself surrounded by a wall of mirrors that fully encompasses you—around, over, and under. The mirrors face out, so the energy that is being directed toward you from another is reflected and goes back to the sender. Your shield is completely sealed, so none of the external energy enters, and, therefore, it has no effect on you. You may feel that it is harsh to send the energy back to the source, but this can actually help the sender to become aware of what he or she is doing, especially if it is an unconscious attack. Spend a few moments feeling the shield form solidly around you. See, sense, and feel the completeness of the shield, and when you can fully sense the shield around you, allow yourself a few moments to be aware of everything that you are experiencing. Now, hold that in place with your intention. For future reference, make a mental note about how your energy appears, how your energy feels, and what your shield looks and feels like. This will make it easy to bring it back into existence again quickly whenever you need it. This shield will go with you wherever you go and will naturally dissipate over time, so repeat this exercise as often as necessary.

Cobalt-Blue Egg Protection Shield

This is another effective energy boundary protection exercise.

Begin by taking in a deep breath, then exhale and relax, releasing any stresses or tensions that you may be feeling. Take in a few more deep, full breaths and focus your mind. Visualize and tangibly feel yourself surrounded by an impenetrable cobalt-blue egg of energy. The energy should appear in your mind's eye to be dynamically vibrating and of even thickness all around you. Make sure that you have spread the energy over your head and under your feet. Your energy is contained within the cobalt-blue egg, so a potentially energy-draining situation is unable to extract it and any attack is unable to reach you through the energy barrier. See, sense, and feel the completeness of the shield, and when you can fully sense the shield around you, allow yourself a few moments to be aware of everything that you are experiencing. Now hold that in place with your intention. For future reference, make a mental note about how your energy appears, how your energy feels, and what your shield looks and feels like. This will make it easy to bring it back into existence again quickly whenever you need it. This shield will go with you wherever you go and will naturally dissipate over time, so repeat this exercise as often as necessary.

Choose Your Own Shield

When creating shields of protection it is sometimes more effective to form an image of your own that is specific to you or the situation that you want to protect yourself from. The Choose Your Own Shield exercise guides you through this process.

Choose one of the protection shield ideas listed previously, or form an image of your own that is specific to you or your situation. Close your eyes, take in a deep breath, and allow yourself to become quiet. Feel

*yourself relax as you inhale and exhale deeply several times. With
mindful focus and intention, think to yourself, "I am placing the shield
of _____ protection around me." Allow your thoughts to soften,
and become aware of all of your senses. Become aware of your powerful
personal energy circulating in your center; see it, feel it, sense it. Now
hold it and keep it in your center as you sense, see, or feel the powerful
energy of your shield around you. Mindfully focus your attention on the
shield. Use all of your mind to sense the shield. Notice what you are
thinking. Use all of your senses to experience the shield, to see the energy
and any color(s), to feel the energy and any color(s), and to tangibly sense
the energy and the color(s) around you. Now hold that in place with your
intention. For future reference, make a mental note about how your energy
appears, how your energy feels, and what your shield looks and feels like.
This will make it easy to bring it back into existence again quickly whenever you need it. This shield will go with you wherever you go and will
naturally dissipate over time, so repeat this exercise as often as necessary.*

Rochele, a friend and client, explains how she uses shielding to help herself stay energetically clean while working. "The Shielding exercise has
been an important part of my daily life. As a manicurist, I deal with
many people on a daily basis. I have been blessed with a full clientele.
Along with monetary support, these people also bring their cares, worries, daily problems, and negativity. Because I work on their hands, these
people emit energy through their hand chakras. Our energy fields tend
to meld, and if I don't shield myself I find I 'soak up' their cares and
worries. As an empathetic and an energy-sensitive individual, this can
greatly affect me. Ideally, I find it best to shield myself first thing in the
morning, before getting on with my day. This provides me with a protective barrier around my aura. Once in place, this shield allows me to
repel another person's troubles and/or energy so that I don't claim it as
my own, so I can be in a place with my own power. There have been
times when I've forgotten to do this before heading off to work, but I've
found this can be done anywhere, in just a few minutes. If I'm working

on a client, I can successfully place this shield around myself mentally without leaving my workstation or the client."

Four Elements Protection Shield

My longtime friend Jason shared the Four Elements Protection Shield with me some time ago, and it has become a special favorite of mine. This is a layered shield. Each layer of the shield draws from a specific element. The order of the elements is as follows: fire, air, water, and earth. Each element and layer of the shield corresponds to a layer of your being. The first, fire, is associated with your heart chakra and corresponds to your passions and your will or drive. Air, the second layer of the shield, is associated with your third-eye chakra and corresponds to your thoughts and knowledge. Water is the third element. It is associated with the chakra in the lower abdomen, and corresponds with movement and action. The fourth element, earth, is associated with your root chakra and corresponds to strength and grounding.

Before you attempt this shielding, make sure you are in a place where you will not be disturbed for a few moments. Take a few moments to relax and release any stress or tension from your day. When you feel calm and centered, picture a circle of fire around you, then take a moment and turn in a circle, seeing and feeling in your mind the flames around you, tracing them with your hands and making them as real to you as you can. The circle of flames can be high, towering flames leaping around you, or a gentler, campfirelike circle of flames around you. Use whatever image makes you feel the safest in your mind. When you have come full circle, stop for a moment and think back on any good memories you have that evoke the warmth of passion or safety. Then, in the air in front of you, trace a circle.

Now you are ready for the second layer. This time you want to think back to all the lessons you have learned in your life, all the knowledge you have gained. Think also of all the things you have learned in this book so far, and as you do so, picture in your mind a circle of wind forming around the circle of fire. Turn in the circle and feel the wind around you; see it fanning the flames of your first circle, feel it against your skin, and imagine all the things you have learned in life being in that wind, forming a protective barrier of knowledge and wisdom between you and the world. Once you have turned full circle, trace in the air in front of you a second, larger circle around the circle you just formed a moment ago.

The third layer is the element of water. Picture in your mind a circle of water forming around the circles of air and fire. See it as a moat that surrounds you. Hear the music of the water as it tumbles and flows in a protective circle around you. Turn in the circle and let the music of the water flow through you; let it carry away the day-to-day stresses of life to leave you refreshed and clean. When you have turned full circle, trace a third, larger circle around the previous two circles that you drew.

Now for earth, the final layer of your shield. This time you want to think of all the things in your life that help to keep you grounded and sane—any friends, family, or support systems of any kind that you have—and around the circle of water, around the circle of air, around the circle of fire, see a square of earth forming around you. It might be mountains or hills, or a hedge or trees forming the square around you. Use whatever feels most comfortable to you, most strong and supportive. See it with your mind, and feel its great strength supporting you.

When you have turned full circle and can feel the strength of the earth with you, trace a square in the air that surrounds the three previous circles that you drew. Now your shield of the elements is complete. Stand within your elemental shielding, relax in the security and strength it offers you, and know that as you go about your day the shield will stay around you, protecting you, ready to shield you and give you strength whenever you need it. See, sense, and feel the completeness of the shield. This shield will go with you wherever you go and will naturally dissipate over time, so repeat this exercise as often as necessary.

Lighted Energy Egg

The Lighted Energy Egg exercise will literally *light you up!* Through visualization and intention, your personal energy will be stimulated to light up, swirl around inside and outside of you, and form a powerful energy boundary. This creates dynamic energy and a natural shield of protection. My favorite candle company makes candles that glow from the inside out when lit. There is a base light that you set the candle of your choice on. It lights up the candle from the inside so you can see how it is going to look when it is lit. This exercise works in a similar fashion, and you get to be the lighted candle. The Lighted Energy Egg exercise is included on the accompanying CD as it is written here.

Relax and release any stress or tension from your mind and body. When you feel calm and centered, picture yourself sitting on top of a round rock with a smooth, flat top. The rock is glowing brightly, and when you sit upon it, it makes you light up and glow. Take a few moments to see, sense, and feel the light glowing through your entire body and energy field. The light inside of you illuminates your energy and looks something like swirling, moist steam wafting out from hot water. Take a few moments to bask in this glow, and simply observe. You may also notice energy holes, leaks, and congestion. These may appear as wisps of smoke escaping from your energy field. Simply notice them for a few moments.

Using your will and intention, begin to stimulate your energy field by stirring the energy of your root chakra located at the base of your torso. After a few moments, send this clear, translucent energy spiraling up the inside of your body. The nourishing energy looks and feels like warm, steamy water bubbling up out of a small internal geyser from your base, as it moves up through the top of your head. Relax and use all of your senses to experience your energy as it continually spirals up your spinal column and billows out through your entire body. Experience the effervescence of your internal geyser for a few moments. When you are ready, allow it to move just beyond the edge of your skin, into the first layer of your energy field. As the energy continues to flow, it grows in strength and dynamism and fills each layer of your energy field, one layer at a time. As each layer clears and energizes, the energy swirls into each layer until reaching the outer boundary.

At the outer boundary, an energy membrane surrounds the layers of your energy field, and you feel it thicken and intensify from the power of your gathering personal energies. This luminescent perimeter appears like a flexible, rubbery eggshell that continues to allow the exchange of gases and energy. Inside your eggshell boundary, your body is the yellow center; the layers of your energy field are the white. Reach out and feel the edges of your energy boundary, and give your luminous eggshell a color that feels right to you. See, sense, feel, and experience it radiating and shimmering in its reclaimed strength and power. This becomes your fortress of protection that allows you to let energy in and out in a healthy way. Inside of your radiant energy boundary, your personal energy nourishes your body and energy field and fills you with vigor and vitality. You are energized.

. . .

At this point, if you have been practicing the energy connecting exercises in the last three chapters, you are probably glowing like a radiant sun. By stimulating your personal energy, clearing away blockages, and fortifying your energy boundaries, you have become accustomed to working with and feeling your own energy. You have experienced the rejuvenating benefits of being aware of energy and learned how to energize yourself when your energy is running low. The beauty of your energy system is that even though it is a closed system that protects you, it is also partially open to allow for energy exchange. In the next chapter you will learn how to access the powerful energizing benefits of connecting with universal life-force energy.

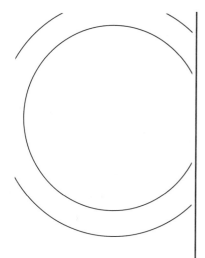

FIVE

Connect with Universal Life-Force Energy

"Aurora Borealis"
Light from above enters on my breath
my Spirit soars
Rooted feet reach deep into the Earth
I am anchored
Mother Earth strength tingles up my legs
stars fill my arms and shoot from my palms
A placid lake glistens
in the moonlight of my belly
the sun radiates from my center
Around my spine swirls a rainbow bridge
another deep breath
I am the dancing aurora borealis
Heaven and Earth live within me
all stress becomes a distant musing
I am in balance ready to live again.
~ Colleen Deatsman

So far, we've learned what energy is, how to amp up our personal life-force energy, and how to clear away the blockages and stop the leakages that drain us. We know that our bodies are designed to be energy converters—closed systems where we can eat a chocolate bar, a salad, or a sirloin steak, and in a short while, *Voila!*, physical energy. We have learned that our personal life-force energy field is made up of wheels and layers of energy that can be consciously stimulated to revitalize and give us more dynamic power.

But is it really a closed system? Wouldn't it be great if we could plug into an exterior source, a limitless wellspring where we could get all the energy we needed to instantly excite and supplement our personal life-force energy? Furthermore, what if that external energy available was of a higher-powered, more refined quality than we are able to produce ourselves?

Fortunately, we *can* plug in to just such an exterior energy source. The answer lies not in the closed system of our bodies, but in the nearly limitless potential of our mind and spirit to be open and receive "universal life-force energy."

WHAT IS UNIVERSAL LIFE-FORCE ENERGY?

Universal life-force energy is a free-flowing, high-vibrational energy that is the foundation of everything. It is omnipresent and is the essence of all things, a subtle undercurrent of all that is. Everything that is, is *alive* with life-force energy. It is the crystal clear, translucent energy force that moves in all things, physical and nonphysical, and is balance and harmony in its most pure form.

Universal life-force energy is the basis of all other energies. It is the impetus to become, and it uses itself to produce that which it is becoming. It remains itself, and morphs itself, densifying and differentiating, to become other manifest forms as well. It is the intelligent raw material that makes up myriad forces of nature, and then, in its varying forms, it is used by them as the building blocks needed to create the infinite diversity existing in the physical and ethereal worlds. Universal life-force energy is both the clay and the hand that shapes it as the universe is molded in each and every moment. It is infinitely creative, conscious, present, and multifaceted. It is all around us. It is below us in the earth, and in everything in the earth, nature, the elements, trees, animals, and air. It is within each of us. Universal life-force energy is in space, clouds, sky, sun, stars, planets, and beyond, into the great void. Cities, shopping malls, this book, and even our dreams have life-force energy flowing through them.

As universal life-force energy works in the energetic and physical universe, it commingles with energies and forms that have already proceeded from it. Like merging ice that floats in water, the manifest universe joins together, along with our own personal life-force energy, to form the web of life that connects all things. This great web is the superstructure that forms an energetic ecosystem where everything works together in harmony—all made of, linked by, and set adrift in the limitless sea of universal life-force energy.

For most people, the world appears to be an ordinary place comprised of a physical environment that can be explained by science. We perceive people and objects as being solid and material. The universal life-force energy that comprises the web of life is a nonordinary world that encompasses, underlies, and runs through this ordinary physical world. The ordinary world is dependent on the web for its life-force energy and existence. The web pervades all of life, is real and present, and, for most people, exists just outside of ordinary perception.

This interconnected web of life-force energy has long been identified by philosophers, scientists, and spiritual authorities, and has been referred to by names such as Subtle Energy, Causal Energy, Prana, Chi, Ki, God, Goddess, Spirit, Universal Power, and Higher Power. It is known to be alive, spirited, animated, and, by many, it is thought to be divine. This is why many religions and spiritual paths describe life-force energy as Deities, Spirit Guides, Ascended Masters, or archetypes with faces, bodies, shapes, forms, and names. Working with these manifestations of the web is a powerful method for healing, guidance, enlightenment, and hope that we will explore in more depth in the next chapter.

In chapter one, we learned how modern technological advances have allowed Western science to analytically prove the existence of this energy field. Quantum physics has determined that this energy not only exists around us, everywhere, all the time, but that it is also a part of us. Leading researchers such as Dr. Gregg Braden tell us that research confirms, "We are permeated with an intelligent field that responds to coherent human emotion."[3] It is also interesting to note that science now believes, as the ancients recorded, that this field of life-force energy has been with us since we began and that we are all related through this single field of energy.

Why Do I Need to Connect with Universal Life-Force Energy?

If this universal life-force energy runs all around us and through us, why aren't we constantly energized?

The ancients figured this out, too.

We have to train ourselves to become receptive. Remember that our bodies and the physical world are the densest constructs of the entire manifest universe. Where the physical body is a dense matter converter that is, (chocolate bar = physical energy), our subtle and causal bodies convert the subtle and causal energies for our use. But, just as when we were children and had to learn how to feed ourselves in order to benefit from solid food, so do we need to learn how to bring in the high-vibrational universal life-force energy in order for us to benefit from it. We have to learn to focus ourselves, allowing the densest parts of us, our body and ego, to step back, and then encourage our subtle and causal selves to be consciously dominant and step to the fore. The degree to which this is effectively done is in direct proportion to the quality and integration of the energies we are able to tap in to.

In other words, we need to open the closed system of the physical and utilize the "higher" parts of ourselves, our subtle and causal bodies, to consciously draw in vibrant universal life-force energy, which we can

3. Gregg Braden, *Speaking the Lost Language of God: Awakening the Forgotten Wisdom of Prayer, Prophecy, and the Dead Sea Scrolls* (Niles, Ill.: Nightingale Conant, 2004).

convert for our own use in promoting our health, revitalizing us, increasing our awareness, and manifesting abundance in our lives.

Why Would I Want to Connect with Universal Life-Force Energy?

Energy and vitality are probably the number one reason why most people would want to connect with universal life-force energy. Because universal life-force energy vibrates at a higher rate than your personal life-force energy, opening up to and receiving this energy powers and amplifies your personal energy. This helps you live with plenty of energy for all the things you need and want to do. When you draw in universal life-force energy you feel power-filled, and this alleviates that run-down, exhausted feeling that so many people endure daily.

Have you noticed that people look older when they are tired and dragging through the day? The tired look and the wrinkles and bags under their eyes seem to become more pronounced. When you are filled with energy and are not so run-down, your eyes sparkle and you have a bounce in your step that makes you look and feel younger. This might seem superficial, but many of us have jobs and responsibilities that require us to be on top of our game. Looking great and feeling vital are important elements for being able to effectively live our lives.

Connecting with universal life-force revitalizes your energy when you become drained. No matter how charmed your life, you are going to experience stress, struggle, and life-draining challenges. Not all energy loss can be prevented, so you must learn how to fuel up when necessary. If you are a person who burns a lot of energy, then you need to fuel up regularly and powerfully throughout the day by accessing universal life-force energy. Unfortunately, most of us are never taught how to access this kind of energetic nourishment, so we struggle along low on energy or only partially refueling by eating or sleeping. The exercises in the how-to section of this chapter will not only help you replenish with energy that heals, they will also help you build protection from energy loss.

When you are energy-filled, you are strong and powerful, and are better suited to handle life challenges. Connecting to something as magnificent as universal life-force energy helps to create an internal strength and positive perspective that make all challenges more manageable. Best of all, there is an infinite amount of life-force energy available. You need only open yourself up to receive this great gift. If you perform the guided journeys, meditations, and exercises found throughout this book whenever you can, and especially when depleted, you can avoid that used-up feeling that victimizes us in the day-to-day world.

Physiologically, universal life-force energy has been proven to help boost physical functioning. Bathing all of the cells in your body in high-vibrational universal life-force energy creates an environment where harmony, healing, and balance reign, even during times of stress. This is not just limited to the body, but also includes mental and emotional health. Direct connection with universal life-force energy helps to clear the energy blockages that cause imbalances that can manifest as depression and anxiety. Every system in your body—your organs, hormones, metabolism, and immune system—will be stronger, healthier, and more vital because perfect health is our natural state when we are in balance. There have been many scientific studies published over recent years that statistically measure the health benefits for individuals participating in activities that transcend the everyday physical world and directly connect one to universal life-force energy. These include prayer, Reiki, meditation, visualization, and shamanic journeying, along with a host of others. One such study by Sandra Harner statistically demonstrates that a boost of the immune system can be accomplished through shamanic journeying. Shamanic journeying is a technique in which the journeyer enters into a trance state and invites his or her soul to travel into the realms of universal life-force energy, thereby directly connecting one's energetic self with this all-pervasive energy.

In much the same way a journeyer connects with universal life-force by sending his or her soul into the subtle worlds, you can invite universal life-force to flow through you here in your everyday world in ordinary reality, boosting your immune system, relieving stress, and healing health concerns. Whether you feel a cold coming on, have a chronic illness, or feel that your energy is blocked, powering up will help bring you back into balance and well-being.

In this chapter you will learn activities that bring universal life-force energy into your body. Many alternative healers use techniques like these to invite this same energy into the body of their client to raise the vibrational rate of their body, mind, emotions, and personal energy field. Inviting this energy in balances the energies of the body, cleanses the body of poisons, and opens and clears stagnant or blocked emotions, behavioral patterns, and personal energy. Free-flowing personal and universal life-force energy help one achieve harmony and balance in their whole being, creating the right circumstances for self-healing.

When we are filled with universal life-force energy we feel centered, balanced, and connected. Connecting with universal life-force energy automatically connects us with our personal life-force energy, even when we feel off-center or under the weather, and this orients us to be engaged and power-filled. We have the power and energy to be fully alive. We feel powerful—not in an aggressive way, but in a calm, peaceful, and centered way. Our personal energy is within us where we can use it. It is not scattered around. We are able to shed our stress and feel composed and stable. This calm, positive stability helps us attract positive people and life circumstances that manifest abundance, prosperity, and well-being in our lives.

Connecting with universal life-force energy is also a high-powered technique to help you break through life struggles and personal growth issues. If you are blocked, stuck, stagnant, feel adrift, or struggling with personal issues or difficult life situations, connecting with universal life-force energy can give perspective, creating shifts in awareness and perception that can help you to grow and make healthy changes. As you overcome self-defeating behaviors and attitudes, you become lighter. These behavioral and perspective shifts allow you to slowly get out of your own way and manifest more clarity and positivity in your daily life. The more you infuse yourself with this insightful and healing universal life-force energy, the more issues you can address and resolve, and objectivity soon replaces confusion. Slowly, you begin to identify with the greater reality of the universe and abandon much of your self-involvement. This increases your awareness still further, and intuition and insight become daily blessings in your life. Enlightenment, the complete under-standing of your place in the universe, is then within easy reach. And it all starts with the simple connection that you will learn here.

Sensing Life-Force Energy and Universal Life-Force Energy

You know that everything in the universe is made up of universal life-force energy at its most basic level. Look at anything, and you are "sens-ing" universal life-force energy. But in order to utilize universal life-force energy for your personal benefit, you need to develop a sense of the subtle manifestations of universal life-force energy, namely, the natural presence of life-force energy.

Throughout this chapter, view the concepts presented as referring to life-force energy on one level, and to universal life-force energy on a deeper, more subtle level. Any time one of the activities asks you to feel or draw in life-force energy, try it first by accessing the life-force energy in the universe of form that surrounds you. You can then try the activities again by reaching deeper and accessing the formless, pervasive universal life-force energy that circulates and underlies this universe of form.

Universal life-force energy, though very powerful, is subtle, and therefore often unseen and unfelt by most people. This is part of the rea-son why it has taken science hundreds of years to confirm its existence. Even without scientific instruments, life-force energy can be seen and felt by those who allow themselves to become relaxed, open, and aware. This actually becomes quite easy for people who have developed their percep-tion. Most people find it easiest to develop this ability to be able to see, sense, and feel energy by becoming quiet inside of themselves.

Relaxation and the conscious silencing of mind chatter are typical avenues for opening to perception. This is achieved through a five-step process: (1) *intention*, your desire to become calm and quiet, (2) *focus*, mindfully directing your attention and placing your thoughts on relax-ing, (3) *releasing*, letting go of mind chatter and your everyday world thoughts, (4) *allowing*, availing yourself to be open to your thoughts, feelings, and sensations to experience energy through any of the thoughts, feelings, or sensations that come to you during this time, and

(5) *accepting*, opening up to and receiving any feelings and information that come to you in this process without judgment.

This is easiest to accomplish in a quiet place where you will not be interrupted. Taking in several long, deep breaths is also helpful for relaxation and calming. Once you become quiet, take in another deep breath and allow yourself to go even deeper into relaxation. When you feel relaxed, open up all of your senses to see, sense, and feel the energy. Because this works so well for most people, I recommend trying to connect with life-force energy in natural locations because nature is an unspoiled physical representation of universal life-force energy.

You have most likely sensed life-force energy, though you may not have been aware of it. Perhaps you sense this energy similar to the ways I do. I am blessed to be able to travel to picturesque northern Michigan each summer to relax in the calm forests and pristine waters of Lake Michigan. The following is a journal entry recorded during one of my trips that describes a moment when I was deeply engaged and sensing the great web and universal life-force energy in nature.

The quiet, clean, fresh air is free from the noises of human life and the boundless sky unencumbered by lights and smog. The long sandy beaches dotted with stones provide much needed solitude from the stresses of my busy life. The occasional sea gull calls, the wind through the trees, and the rhythmic lapping of the waves as they caress the shore are the only sounds I hear. The power of the great lake permeates my awareness, even though today her layers of turquoise changing to deep blue are calm. The gentle rhythms reach into my body and soul and move deep in my center. All of my senses validate the universal life-force energy within me. I feel peaceful, powerful, and connected to the beauty around and within me. Between the two islands on the horizon I see minute bubbles forming tiny winding formless images against the azure sky. The vision seems surreal, but I know that I have opened my senses into the realm of energy. Lost for many moments, the growling of my stomach reminds me that it is time to build the campfire to prepare my dinner back at camp. Later that night, snuggled in my sleeping bag, the rhythm and the images continue to move through me as I drift off to sleep.

Now it's your turn. Take a few moments right now to sit back, take in a deep breath, and relax. Imagine yourself in one of your favorite places in nature, perhaps a park, garden, forest, ocean, or lake. Recall the feelings that you have while in this place, and allow yourself to really feel them now. Take as much time as you can.

If it was difficult for you to sense energy during this exercise, that's okay. What now may seem abstract and difficult to understand can be seen, sensed, and felt in tangible ways through the activities that follow.

How to Connect with Life-Force Energy

In order to see, sense, feel, connect with, and utilize life-force energy, we must become open, perceptive, and receptive. These are skills that can be honed with practice. When first beginning to awaken your energy-sensing abilities, you will experience the most success when you are relaxed and quiet physically, mentally, and emotionally.

Choose a place or an object that you would like to use as a focal point for sensing life-force energy. Set your intention to relax. Take in a deep breath, clear your mind, and relax your body. Once you have become relaxed, mentally focus your intention on sensing the energy in the place, object, or empty space. Release your mind chatter, and allow your mind and emotions to become quiet. Intentionally open up all of your senses, allowing yourself to feel, visualize, and perceive. When you are ready, receive this energy by allowing it to flow into you and through you. Take in a deep breath and open your body, mind, chakras, and personal energy field. Consciously draw in the energy without judgment or conditions, accepting everything that you notice and feel. Do this for as long as you have time. When you are finished, don't shut back down. Try to stay open for as long as you can, and remain aware of the different sensations you are having.

When developing your perception and reception skills, keep in mind that you will experience the most success in places where you can relax and where life-force energy is abundant. Your soft room is one of those places. Finding places in nature without distractions may also be favorable because nature and natural environments are perfect expressions of universal life-force energy. Soon you will be able to perceive and receive life-force energy no matter where you are using your intention and awareness.

The following guided journey, meditation, and exercises will help you hone your skills of sensing, perceiving, and receiving universal life-force energy by employing the five-step process of intention, focus, releasing, allowing, and accepting. The Sacred Healing Medicine Place guided journey is included on the accompanying CD as it is written here, in its entirety.

GUIDED JOURNEY

Sacred Healing Medicine Place

Go to a soft space where you will not be disturbed, and turn off all telephones. If indoors, dim the lights and play relaxing music, if you'd like. Sit or lie down where you will feel warm and comfortable, safe and protected. Take a moment to quiet yourself. Take in a deep breath and relax. Allow your eyes to naturally close. Take a few moments to cleanse your energy field using the Rainbow Waterfall exercise (page 63). After several moments of clearing allow yourself to soften into deep relaxation.

Let go of any worries or stresses. Know that right now, there is nowhere else to go and nothing else to do. Relax and enjoy this time for yourself. Take in a long, deep breath, and feel the air nurture your lungs. As you exhale, allow all of your stresses and tensions to release. With each inhalation, you feel clear, pure energy entering your lungs and spreading throughout your body. With each exhalation, you feel any toxins, discomfort, or pain exiting your body with the breath. Allow your mind to relax as the muscles of your body melt deeply into the place where you are sitting or lying. Feel supported and cradled by the earth, floor, chair, couch, or bed. With your next inhalation and exhalation, allow your body to fully relax, feeling at peace. Allow any thoughts to flow through you, acknowledge them, and then let them drift away, like balloons floating high into the sky. Your mind relaxes, and your brain becomes a quiet, distant observer.

As you continue to relax, imagine that you are walking down a path in the woods, feeling light and connected with nature. It's a beautiful day, filled with soft sunlight and a warm, gentle breeze. Use all of your senses to experience the universal life-force energy, and enjoy your connection with Mother Earth. As you stroll down this path in the woods, notice birds flying from tree to tree. Deeply breathe the fresh forest air. As you walk along the path, the woods slowly open up into a heavenly meadow filled with wildflowers of all colors. Notice the bees and the butterflies as they float among the flowers. Slowly wander through this heavenly meadow, feeling calm and connected. Use all of your senses to feel the beautiful universal life-force energy. As you continue, the path comes to a stone stairway, leading down to a large rock archway. There are ten wide and flat steps, and each stone is easy to step on. With each number, imagine yourself taking one step down. With every step you take, go further and further into deep relaxation. One, take the first step; two, take the second; three; four, going down deeper and deeper; five; six, more and more relaxed; seven; eight, deeply relaxed; nine; ten. As you reach the bottom, you walk underneath the rock archway and discover your own sacred healing medicine place. This is the most magnificent place in all of creation. Using all of your senses, take a few moments to explore your sacred healing medicine place. Notice that you feel calm, safe, and serene. No one else may enter here without an invitation from you. As you continue to explore this extraordinary place, you are drawn to a comfortable area. Go to that place. Sit or lie down, and become totally relaxed.

Breathe deeply of the healing life-force energy of this sacred place. As you continue to relax, feel the strength and the power of your sacred heal-

ing medicine place. Let it fill you with the potent healing energy of the universal life-force. Feel this energy connecting with and stimulating your own personal energy. Feel power and vibrancy returning to your body and soul. You are strong, happy, and healthy. Feel your vibrant inner sun dancing within your center. See and feel yourself full of energy and living life to the fullest. See and feel yourself filled with the energy of the universal life-force. Every cell of your body is saturated with this glowing, healing, revitalizing life-force energy. You are filled with energy and passion for life. Your body is warm and healthy, and growing stronger each moment. You are connected with your own internal wisdom. Your body, mind, emotions, and soul are nurtured in pure harmony and balance.

Take in a deep breath. Allow the life-force energy to deepen within your body and soul. Feel the vibrations growing stronger and stronger within you, with every breath that you take, and every beat of your heart. With each passing moment, your essence absorbs the life-force energy, and you grow profoundly.

Becoming aware that it is time to return to your normal activities, you gently rise up from your special spot, coming slowly to sitting, then kneeling, and then carefully to standing. You slowly walk through your sacred healing medicine place, breathing deeply of all the powerful life-force energy. As you reach the large rock archway, turn to look once more into your beautiful sacred healing medicine place. Gathering one last deep breath of this healing, calm, peaceful power, you step through the large rock archway. With every number that you count, you become more awake and more alert. Ten, begin ascending the steps; nine, take the second; eight; seven; six, coming up; five; four; three, becoming more awake; two; one. Welcome back to your body. You are fully awake and alert. You feel better than you have in a long time.

Sit quietly for a few moments and reflect on your experience. Be gentle with yourself as you wiggle and stretch, becoming fully present in your body and conscious mind. Fully express your experience, thoughts, and feelings in your journal.

MEDITATION

Open to Receive and Perceive Life-Force Energy in Nature

Practicing meditation in nature to sense and perceive universal life-force energy can provide you with a direct link to this source because nature is a perfect expression of universal life-force energy at work. This is evidenced by nature's regenerating characteristics. All places in nature that are destroyed will eventually renew. There are locations all around the world where the land has been depleted, destroyed, and devastated by mining and pollution. Walk away from any one of these lifeless, barren spots and then return in twenty-five years, and you will find a thriving and renewed ecosystem in that very place. That is universal life-force energy in action.

In nature we can also find the solitude that helps us to quiet our minds and slow down our busyness so that we can relax, receive, and perceive universal life-force energy. Most people feel calm, peaceful, and rejuvenated after a day in the woods, at the beach, or in a park or a garden, not only because there is a reduction in stress, but also because they have connected with life-force energy. If you have a favorite place that you like to go to that makes you feel good, or one that shines in your childhood memories, you have found a personal power place. These are places where your soul resonates with the universal life-force. Spending time in power places helps you to energize and heal. They are also great places to begin to open up to and receive universal life-force energy.

Another way that we perceive life-force energy is in the elements: air, water, fire, and earth. Nature is composed of the subtle energies of the elements. A gentle waterfall, a babbling brook, a peaceful lake, and a roaring ocean are manifestations of the element of water. The warm summer sun, an explosive volcano, and a flash of lightning are manifestations of the element of fire. A raging tornado, a gentle breeze, and the whisper of wind through the pines are manifestations of the element of air. A stoic mountain, sparkling crystals, and warm, squishy mud are manifestations of the element of earth. In your meditation you may find that in many places the energies of the elements come together.

The sun heats and circulates the gentle currents of air. The water of the ocean mixes with air on a breeze and becomes mist that sprays onto the earth of the sandy beach. As you perform this meditation, you will find that places and elements have their own energy and universal life-force energy. Your mission during this meditation is to visualize, sense, and feel all of these energies and begin to recognize how they all work together to form harmony and balance, health and well-being. Notice how all energies, including your personal energy, mix and blend and become a part of the web of universal life-force energy. Explore the power of the intermingling of energies, for it is this very intermingling that silhouettes universal life-force energy against the canvas of nature.

Choose a place in nature where you feel comfortable—perhaps your power place if you have one. You can either be physically present in that place, or you can travel to that place in your mind. If you can do this exercise outdoors in the energy that you are attempting to connect with, that may make it more real for you. However, since we have the power to send our minds anywhere we wish, it is not necessary to physically be in the place you have chosen.

Sit in quiet contemplation in your nature place, or in a soft space where you will not be disturbed. Open your mind and relax. Observe, notice, experience, and feel everything about that place. Focus your attention on your feelings and opening up all of your senses to experience the place you have chosen. Allow any distracting thoughts to drift away. Notice them and let them go.

Continue to sit quietly, and observe the place you have chosen for a while. See and feel, or imagine and feel, everything about the place you have chosen. What do you see? What do you smell? What do you feel physically? What do you feel emotionally? What do you sense? Is there any movement? What elements do you notice? Is the wind blowing or the sun shining? Do any of the elements blend together? Relax and soften your eyes, and continue to observe for a while. Allow yourself to sense and feel the universal life-force energy of this place. Allow yourself to sense and feel all of the objects in this place. Allow yourself to sense and feel the empty space in between. Allow yourself to sense and feel the energies that are the objects and the spaces. Sense and feel the energy that is all three. Breathe deeply of this energy. Notice your sensations.

Now close your eyes, and allow your inner wisdom to bubble forth. Relax, focus, and feel. Open up to feeling all of the energy around and in this place, including your own. Sense and feel the space between you and this place. Sense and feel the space between you and all of the objects in this place. Sense and feel the energy in that space. Sense and feel your own energy. Does your energy feel differently here? Allow questions and answers to form in and out of your thoughts. Questions like: Does the combination of the elements and other energies affect this place? Is this place alive? Do the objects in this place have a soul? Does this place have any energy or a soul? Does it have a spirit? Are the soul and spirit the same thing, or something different? Is this universal life-force energy? Is universal life-force energy different from the energy of this place? Is universal life-force energy different from the energy of the objects in this place? Is universal life-force energy different from other kinds of energy? If so, how? How can you tell?

Stay in this place in contemplation for as long as you have time, asking your own questions of yourself. When you are ready, take in a deep breath and allow yourself a few moments to shift your awareness back to ordinary life and fully integrate back into your body.

EXERCISES TO CONNECT WITH LIFE-FORCE ENERGY

The following exercises utilize the five-step process to connect you with life-force energy and can be performed anywhere and at any time since it is not necessary for you to enter into an altered state of consciousness. If you have the time and are in an appropriate place, for added relaxation and receptivity you may choose to enter into an altered state of consciousness, as described in chapter two, before performing these exercises. If so, use your favorite relaxation technique or the Universal

Induction described in chapter 1. Once you have eased yourself into relaxation, begin the exercise while maintaining your inner stillness.

Opening

Our first energy connecting exercise is a resting exercise called Opening.

Lie down or sit comfortably with palms facing up, ready to receive. Take in a deep breath and allow your mind to relax. Focus your attention on the soles of your feet. Feel your feet open and consciously draw life-force energy from everything around you in through them. Focus and feel the warmth and tingling. Focus and feel for a few more moments. When you are ready, focus your attention on your solar plexus. Feel your center open and consciously draw in life-force energy from everything around you. Focus and feel. When you are ready, focus your attention on the palms of your hands. Feel your palms open and consciously draw life-force energy from everything around you in through them. Focus and feel the warmth and tingling. Focus and feel for a few more moments. When you are ready, focus your attention on the top (crown) of your head. Feel your crown open and consciously draw in life-force energy from everything around you. Focus and feel. Tune in to all of these places in your body simultaneously: the soles of your feet, the center of your torso, and the crown of your head. Feel them open, and use all of your senses to feel the energy coming together inside of you. Feel it swirl as it mixes together, and mindfully stir it. Spread this delicious mix of universal life- force energy throughout your body and hold it. Notice what this life-force energy feels like. Notice any colors that you may feel, sense, and perceive. Notice any physical sensations that you may feel, sense, and perceive. Notice any emotions that you may feel, sense, and perceive. Notice any thoughts that you may feel, sense, and perceive. Notice what this feels like on the surface of your body. Notice what this feels like inside of your body. Notice what this feels like deep in the core of your body. Do this for as long as you have time. When you are finished, don't shut back down.

Try to stay open for as long as you can, and remain aware of the different sensations you are having.

Gathering of Life-Force Energy

The Gathering of Life-Force Energy exercise is a quick and powerful energy movement exercise that is sure to energize you on all levels. It is an exercise that uses physical movement, in addition to the five-step process to gather energy to connect you with life-force energy.

Stand with your feet hip-distance apart, arms down at your sides. Relax, loosen the muscles in your face, and soften your eyes. Take in a deep breath, hold it for a moment, and empty all the thoughts out of your mind with your exhalation. Take in another deep breath and raise your arms, palms up from your sides, in a slow, mindful sweeping motion all the way over your head, gathering in the universal life-force energy of your surroundings and the infinite universe. Turn your palms down and bring your arms down the front of your body, sinking the energy into your body, and then deep into your solar plexus and root center. Hold your hands here for a few moments and breathe naturally. Focus and feel. Be aware of how you feel emotionally. Be aware of how you feel physically. Be aware of how you feel mentally. Be aware of how you feel spiritually. Be aware of how your whole energy field feels. Repeat in multiples of three. Continue to empty your mind of thoughts. Relax, and try to be aware of nothing other than how the universal life-force energy affects you, how it feels inside of your energy field, and how it feels inside of your whole being. Consciously draw the energy in and notice how you feel. Do this for as long as you have time. When you are finished, don't shut back down. Try to stay open for as long as you can, and remain aware of the different sensations you are having.

Strong Mountain

A common malady of our technological world is a shift from right-brained, intuitive living to left-brained, logical living. In so doing we spend the vast majority of our energy on mental processes. This causes our personal energy to be up in our head and leaves us feeling disconnected from our body, emotions, and soul. Without awareness and conscious effort to bring universal life-force energy down into our whole being, we end up feeling scattered, energetically unbalanced, and "ungrounded." This next exercise will help you to become grounded, a term used to describe the conscious act of reconnecting with universal life-force energy and anchoring it in the whole body.

The Strong Mountain exercise can be used daily as part of your set ritual, as well as anytime during the day that you feel scattered, unbalanced, or disconnected. It is especially powerful to practice this outdoors if you can, but it is equally effective indoors.

Clear yourself of blockages and negative energy by using your favorite activity from chapter 3. Stand with your feet hip-distance apart, arms down at your sides. Imagine in your mind that you are becoming a strong mountain. See and feel the soles of your feet opening to the Earth. Imagine that your feet are strongly connected to the Earth. Your feet are a part of the Earth. See and feel the solid rock growing out of the bottom of your feet reaching deep into the core of the Earth. Use all of your senses to feel the Earth—the many layers, temperature changes, and texture of the soil and rock as it changes down through the layers. See and feel the solid rock of your feet going deep down through the water table and beyond to the core depths of the Earth. Breathe in deeply of the life-force energy from Mother Earth. Bring this energy up through your feet and legs, imagining them to be the base of the strong mountain. Feeling the strength of your base, move the life-force Earth energy up into your torso, imagining it to be the center of the mountain. Visualize, sense, and feel the Earth's life-force energy mingle with your personal energy as you become the mountain essence. Feeling solid and strong, look up and raise

your arms and hands, palms up. Feel the universal life-force energy of the
sky and the infinite universe as you imagine your arms and head to be
the peak of the strong mountain. Draw the universal life-force energy
from above into your hands, arms, and head as you bring your palms
together over your head, forming a pinnacle. Visualize, sense, and feel the
life-force energy flow down through your hands, arms, and head into the
heart and center of your mountain. Visualize, sense, and feel the energy
mingle and mix with your personal essence and the Earth's life-force
energy. Breathe deeply, feel deeply. Become the strong mountain. Your
base reaches deep into the Earth; your torso is the center and heart of the
mountain; your head, arms, and hands reach high into the sky, connect-
ing all of the universal life-force energies together within your body. As
this magnificent mountain, see and feel yourself vibrating with the power
of life. Allow yourself to hold this image and feeling for a few moments.
Consciously draw the energy in for as long as you have time. When you
are finished, don't shut back down. Try to stay open for as long as you
can, and remain aware of the different sensations you are having.

Energy Boost

The Energy Boost exercise is similar to the Personal Energy Boost exercise you learned in chapter 2, with an additional step of intentionally bringing in universal life-force energy to help you stimulate your personal energy and empower it with universal life-force energy.

Begin by taking in a deep breath and relaxing. Place your open palms
down, hands on top of, or just above, the top of your head. Hold this
position while focusing the power of your mind on the color violet and
feeling your personal energy. Now, with your intention, draw universal
life-force energy into the area with your breath. Do this by taking in a
deep breath and sending the energy to the space beneath your hands.
Breathe deeply, bringing in more energy, and use all of your senses to feel

the energy. After a few moments, move your hands down to cover your third eye (forehead) and the back of your head. Hold, focus on the color indigo, and feel your personal energy. With your intention, draw universal life-force energy into the area with your breath. Take in a deep breath, and send the energy to the space between your hands. Breathe deeply, bringing in more energy, and use all of your senses to feel the energy. Move to your throat center, placing your hands just above the body in the front and back of your neck. Hold, focus on the color blue, and feel your personal energy. With your intention, draw universal life-force energy into the area. Take in a deep breath, and send the energy to the space between your hands. Breathe deeply, bringing in more energy, and use all of your senses to feel the energy. Move to your heart center, placing both of your hands on your chest. Hold, focus on the color green, and feel your personal energy. With your intention, draw universal life-force energy into the area. Take in a deep breath and send the energy to the space beneath your hands. Breathe deeply, bringing in more energy, and use all of your senses to feel the energy. Move to the solar plexus, placing one hand on the front and one hand on the back center of your being. Hold, focus on the color yellow, and feel your personal energy. Draw universal life-force energy into the area by taking in a deep breath and sending the energy to the space between your hands. Breathe deeply, bringing in more energy, and use all of your senses to feel the energy. Move to the spleen center, placing one hand on your abdomen and one hand on your lower back. Hold, focus on the color orange, and feel your personal energy. With your intention, draw universal life-force energy into the area by taking in a deep breath and sending the energy to the space between your hands. Breathe deeply, bringing in more energy, and use all of your senses to feel the energy. Move to the root center, placing one hand just above the body of your genital area and the other on your derriere. Hold, focus on the color red, and feel your personal energy. With your intention, draw universal life-force energy into the area. Take in a deep breath, and send the energy to the space between your hands. Breathe deeply, bringing in more energy, and use all of your senses to feel the energy. In one fluid movement, take your hands to the floor and sweep up the universal life-force energy of the Earth with your hands open, fingers together, palms facing your body. Bring your hands all the way up your body from the floor to above your head while visualizing the rainbow colors of your chakras. Feel and receive the energy flow for as long as you have time. When you are finished, don't shut back down. Try to stay open for as long as you can, and remain aware of the different sensations you are having.

Inversion Awareness

You learned steps one through four of the Inversion Awareness Energy exercise in chapter 2. In this chapter you will add step 5 to draw in universal life-force energy.

Step 1: *Sweep all of your personal and mental energy inside of yourself. Extend your arms out at your sides and sweep your arms up over your head. Pull your personal energy from your energy field outside of yourself down to the inside of your head. Blend your personal energy with your consciousness, concentration, attention, intention, and mental energy. Pull all of this energy through your head and neck into your heart chakra. Hold the energy here, and be aware of the vibrations and feelings it brings. Hold for a while. Feel. Sense. When ready, pull it down deeper into your center and hold it; be aware of the vibrations and the wisdom it brings.*

Step 2: Sweep the energy of the sun inside of yourself. Extend your arms out at your sides and sweep your arms up over your head. Pull life-giving energy from the sun down inside of your body. Pull this powerful energy in through your head and neck into your heart chakra. Hold the energy here, and allow the light of the sun to illuminate your emotions and feelings, shedding light on the awareness and insights felt in step one. Hold for a while. Feel. Sense. When ready, pull it down deeper into your center and hold it. Allow the light of the sun to illuminate your wisdom and the energy of your soul. Hold for a while. When ready, anchor your personal energy and the energy of the sun into the Earth through your root chakra. In your root chakra see, sense, and feel the energies blending into a radiant swirling rainbow.

Step 3: Bridge this energy from bottom to top by sending swirling rainbow sparkling electric energy from chakra to chakra up your spinal column and body from your root chakra to your center. Hold. When ready send this energy up your spinal column and body from your center to your heart chakra. Hold. When ready send this energy up your spinal column and body from your heart chakra to your head. Hold. Feel the power! Sense the energy!

Step 4: When the internal bridge is complete, expand the swirling rainbow sparkling electric energy from the core of the inside of your body out into your whole energy field, inside and outside of your body. Hold. Feel the power! Sense the energy!

Step 5: In your mind, imagine that you are in a power place in nature, or journey to your sacred healing medicine place. Feel the personal power and awareness that you have inside of yourself from steps one through four. Now draw the life-force energy of this powerful place inside of yourself. Extend your arms out at your sides and sweep your arms up over your head, pulling the energy down through the inside of your head and neck into your heart chakra. Hold the energy here, and be aware of the vibrations and feelings it brings into your being. When you feel ready, pull it down deeper into your center and hold it. Be aware of all of your sensations. When ready, pull it down deep into your body, grounding it in your root chakra. Allow yourself to vibrate power and wisdom. Notice how you feel.

Continue the energy flow for as long as you have time. When you are finished, don't shut back down. Try to stay open for as long as you can, and remain aware of the different sensations you are having.

Rainbow Fountain of Energy

The Rainbow Fountain of Energy exercise entails drawing in universal life-force energy from the Earth and the infinite universe and moving it through your body and energy field, creating a fountain of flowing energy. This exercise not only connects us with universal life-force energy, it also stimulates our personal energy, clears energy blockages, seals energy leakages, and naturally provides a shield of energetic protection around us. This exercise leaves one feeling whole, centered, and energized.

Begin by standing with your feet hip-distance apart, arms down at your sides. Close your eyes, and take in a deep breath. Keep breathing deeply throughout the exercise, using your breath, physical movement, and intention to draw in and move the energy. Allow yourself to relax; perhaps slip into an altered state of consciousness if you choose. Place your attention on the soles of your feet and the crown of your head. Take in a deep breath, bend over, and draw in the strong, grounding energy of the Earth. Feel it slowly moving up your feet and legs and into your base chakra as you roll back up and place your hands on your root chakra. Raise your arms above your head. Take in a deep breath, and draw in the universal life-force energy from above as you bring your hands down over your head and face. Feel the energy melting in through the top of your head and flowing down into your root chakra as you bring your hands down over your body and place them on your root chakra. Where these two energies meet, see the chakra ignite with a deep, vibrant red energy. See, sense, and feel that red ball of energy grow and expand, becoming a radiant source of glowing, ruby red light that begins to saturate all of the tissues in your body. See, sense, and feel this light soaking into your abdomen, chest, head, and out your arms, bathing organs, muscle, blood, and bone until your entire body becomes a great neon beacon of this light. After a few moments, allow that ruby energy to recede once again back to its home in your base chakra, where it continues to glow and spin brightly.

Take in a deep breath, bend over, and draw in the strong, grounding energy of the Earth. Feel it slowly moving up your feet and legs and into your sacral chakra as you roll back up and place your hands on your sacral chakra. Raise your arms above your head. Take in a deep breath, and draw in the universal life-force energy from above as you bring your hands down over your head and face. Feel the energy melting in through the top of your head and flowing down into your sacral chakra as you bring your hands down over your body and place them on your sacral chakra. The two energies combine, spin, and glow here with a bright orange light. See, sense, and feel that orange ball of energy grow and expand, becoming a radiant source of glowing, bright orange light that begins to saturate all of the tissues in your body. See, sense, and feel this light soaking into your abdomen, chest, head, and out your arms, bathing organs, muscle, blood, and bone until your entire body becomes a great neon beacon of this light. Stir this energy and expand it throughout your body, saturating every cell with this orange, regenerative light. After a few moments, shrink the light back to its home in your second chakra, where it continues to spin and glow a brilliant orange.

Take in a deep breath, bend over, and draw in the strong, grounding energy of the Earth. Feel it slowly moving up your feet and legs and into your solar plexus as you roll back up and place your hands on your solar plexus. Raise your arms above your head. Take in a deep breath, and draw in the universal life-force energy from above as you bring your hands down over your head and face. Feel the energy melting in through the top of your head and flowing down into your solar plexus as you bring your hands down over your body and place them on your solar plexus. The two energies combine, spin, and glow here with a deep golden light. See, sense, and feel that golden ball of energy grow and expand, becoming a radiant source of glowing, deep gold light that begins to saturate all of the tissues in your body. See, sense, and feel this light soaking into your abdomen, chest, head, and out your arms, bathing organs, muscle, blood, and bone until your entire body becomes a great neon beacon of this light. Stir this energy and expand it throughout your body, saturating every cell with this golden, regenerative light. After a few moments, shrink the light back to its home in your solar plexus, where it continues to spin and glow a deep gold.

Take in a deep breath, bend over, and draw in the strong, grounding energy of the Earth. Feel it slowly moving up your feet and legs and into your heart chakra as you roll back up and place your hands on your heart chakra. Raise your arms above your head. Take in a deep breath, and draw in the universal life-force energy from above as you bring your hands down over your head and face. Feel the energy melting in through the top of your head and flowing down into your heart chakra as you bring your hands down over your body and place them on your heart chakra. The two energies combine, spin, and glow here with an emerald green. See, sense, and feel that emerald green ball of energy grow and expand, becoming a radiant source of glowing, emerald green light which begins to saturate all of the tissues in your body. See, sense and feel this light soaking into your abdomen, chest, head, and out your arms, bathing organs, muscle, blood, and bone until your entire body becomes a great neon beacon of this light. Stir this energy and expand it throughout your body, saturating every cell with this emerald green, regenerative light. After a few moments, shrink the light back to its home in your heart chakra, where it continues to spin and glow an emerald green.

Take in a deep breath, bend over, and draw in the strong, grounding energy of the Earth. Feel it slowly moving up your feet and legs and into your throat chakra as you roll back up and place your hands on your throat chakra. Raise your arms above your head. Take in a deep breath, and draw in the universal life-force energy from above as you bring your hands down over your head and face. Feel the energy melting in through the top of your head and flowing down into your throat chakra as you bring your hands down over your head and place them on your throat chakra. The two energies combine, spin, and glow here with a deep azure blue. See, sense, and feel that azure blue ball of energy grow and expand, becoming a radiant source of glowing, deep azure blue light that begins to saturate all of the tissues in your body. See, sense, and feel this light soaking into your abdomen, chest, head, and out your arms, bathing organs, muscle, blood, and bone until your entire body becomes a great neon beacon of this light. Stir this energy and expand it throughout your body, saturating every cell with this azure blue, regenerative light. After a few moments, shrink the light back to its home in your throat chakra, where it continues to spin and glow a deep azure blue.

Take in a deep breath, bend over, and draw in the strong, grounding energy of the Earth. Feel it slowly moving up your feet and legs and into your third-eye chakra as you roll back up and place your hands on your third-eye chakra. Raise your arms above your head. Take in a deep breath, and draw in the universal life-force energy from above as you bring your hands down over your head. Feel the energy melting in through the top of your head and flowing down into your third-eye chakra as you bring your hands down over your third-eye chakra. The two energies combine, spin, and glow here with an indigo purple light. See, sense, and feel that indigo ball of energy grow and expand, becoming a radiant source of glowing, deep indigo light that begins to saturate all of the tissues in your body. See, sense, and feel this light soaking into your abdomen, chest, head, and out your arms, bathing organs, muscle, blood, and bone until your entire body becomes a great neon beacon of this light. Stir this energy and expand it throughout your body, saturating every cell with this indigo, regenerative light. After a few moments, shrink the light back to its home in your third-eye chakra, where it continues to spin and glow a deep indigo purple.

Take in a deep breath, bend over, and draw in the strong, grounding energy of the Earth. Feel it slowly moving up your feet and legs and into your crown chakra as you roll back up and place your hands on your crown chakra. Raise your arms above your head. Take in a deep breath, and draw in the universal life-force energy from above as you bring your hands down to the top of your head. Feel the energy melting down into your crown chakra. The two energies combine, spin, and glow here with a pale violet light. See, sense, and feel that violet ball of energy grow and expand, becoming a radiant source of glowing, pale violet light that begins to saturate all of the tissues in your body. See, sense and feel this light soaking into your abdomen, chest, head, and out your arms, bathing organs, muscle, blood, and bone until your entire body becomes a great neon beacon of this light. Stir this energy and expand it throughout your body, saturating every cell with this violet, regenerative light. After a few moments, shrink the light back to its home in your crown chakra, where it continues to spin and glow a pale violet.

When all seven chakras have been energized, continue to see and feel them spinning and glowing in each of their homes, washing and energizing all of your tissues. See, sense, and feel the swirling bright light of the universal life-force surrounding your body. See, sense, and feel the swirling maroon of the Earth energy beneath you. On your next inhalation, draw the bright light and maroon of the universal and Earth energies into your body and chakras. As the universal and Earth energies blend with your chakra energies, a radiant, internal rainbow glows in the center of your body extending from your feet to your head.

Using your breath, body movement, and intention, reach down, and as you inhale deeply, draw the rainbow energy up through your feet, legs, and body as you roll up to standing, place your hands on your solar plexus and exhale. On your next inhalation, sweep your hands and arms up over your body and over your head, drawing the rainbow energy through your body and head. As you exhale, let the rainbow energy flow out the top of your head like a water fountain and spill down around you as you sweep your arms out and down to your sides. See, sense, and feel the power of the colorful energies gushing up through your body like an internal geyser. As the energy exits your head, see, sense, and feel rainbow droplets cascade out to the limits of your energy field and down again to your feet. As the rainbow droplets mist through your energy field, see, sense, and feel your energy field and body being cleansed and refreshed by the movement of this energy. Continue drawing up the rainbow energy at your own pace using your inhalations, body movements, and intention. Feel the cleansing, power-filling action of the rainbow energy moving up through your body and head. Feel it spill out into your energy field and back to the earth on your exhalations. Repeat at least six times, and continue the energy movement until your body, and the luminous egg that is your energy field, are completely energized.

The Rainbow Fountain of Energy exercise is a very popular and frequently used exercise because of its wide-ranging benefits. Rochele shares, "The rainbow fountain has played an important role in my self-healing. This exercise can be done in a matter of minutes and it provides grounding, centering, chakra balancing, and connection with the universal life-force energy. Most importantly, it connects me with the Divine Force and opens me to greater awareness. I do the Rainbow Fountain exercise when I first notice I'm feeling tired, disconnected, stressed, or anxious. It allows me to prioritize daily events by slowing down and connecting with Spirit while taking a personal inventory of my feelings."

· · ·

Combining the energy exercises you have learned so far is a powerful way for you to individualize your power-filling regime. By combining any of the activities described in this book or others you may have already been practicing, you can fill with universal life-force energy on a very deep level. Be creative and allow your intuition to be your guide as you experiment and blend the combinations that are most effective for you.

· · ·

Perceiving, receiving, and connecting with life-force energy and universal life-force energy would not be complete without addressing the consciousness, spirituality, and divinity inherent in this intelligent energy. Chapter 6 will take us through this exploration.

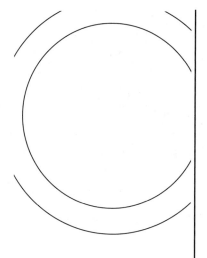

SIX

Divine Spiritual Energy

By the very fact that you call upon God,
the archangels, the invisible ones of Creation,
then they are there.
They will always be there,
and in our petition,
we become aware of them.
~Mark Stavish, The Path of Alchemy

Now that you have experienced the vibrant power of universal life-force energy, you can appreciate the benefits of regularly filling with this high vibrational energy. You know the techniques to use to plug in so that you get all the energy you need to instantly activate your personal life-force energy. You have also learned that bathing your body and energy field with these high-powered vibrations frequently is the key to reestablishing and maintaining exceptional energy and health.

But what if this energy had a particular energetic signature, a name, or perhaps a form that you could see, sense, feel, and invoke during times of need? An identity that would help you associate with it that makes it more personal and tangible? Well, it does. Some of the most resplendent energies that we can interact with are universal life-force energies that coalesce into beings and forces of significant spiritual and religious importance to us. The energy that we can embody by tapping into this endless source is powerful beyond measure.

WHAT ARE DIVINE SPIRITUAL ENERGIES, DEITIES, AND SPIRIT GUIDES?

As you may recall, the high-powered universal life-force energy that you have been accessing is a free-flowing, high vibrational energy that is the foundation of everything. It is omnipresent and is the essence of all things, the creator and the subtle undercurrent of the entire web of life.

This interconnected web of life-force energy is known to be alive, spirited, animated, conscious, intelligent, and, by many, is thought to be divine. Since the beginning of human consciousness there has been a universal need to identify this force, and philosophers, scientists, and spiritual authorities have long been referring to it by names that imply a divine or spiritual power—names such as God, Goddess, Spirit, Universal Power, Higher Power, Universal Source, The Great Web of Life, The Great Spirit, The Holy Spirit, The Great Mystery, Lord, Lady, Mother/Father God, Allah, Prana, Chi, Ki, The Light, The Source, The Divine, Subtle Energy, Causal Energy, and the list goes on. Multitudes of people have argued and fought over the names for centuries, but beyond the philosophies and dogmas is a life-force energy that lives within each of us, regardless of what we call it. It is the Spirit that moves in all living things, and that brings all things to life.

Many people have strong preferences and opinions about religious and spiritual issues and, indeed, devastating wars have been fought, and continue to be fought, over this very thing. Before we go any further, I want to point out that the purpose of this chapter is to help you connect with the powerful energies of spiritual and divine universal power. The intention is not to have a religious discussion or to debate dogmas or beliefs. Plain and simple, Spirit is a manifestation of universal life-force energy, and it is a powerful source that we can connect with. The focus is not to discuss religion, but to teach you how to tap in to the powerhouse of spiritual universal life-force energy effectively with reverence and honor.

Generally, the names listed above depict a vast energy that is without form. Some are given anthropomorphic forms so that they become more real to us, like the white-haired man in the sky called God, but realistically, energies of higher magnitude, even if they are distinct entities in the etheric realms, have no need for a conventional body as we would imagine it. So, when we refer to the divine or spiritual omnipotent energy, what we are talking about is a force, an intelligence, an energy that is formless and omnipresent. We refer to this as causal energy, and it is the highest level of vibrational energy.

Many religions and spiritual paths teach that the all-pervading divine life-force energy has "helper" energies that interact with us and act as a bridge to connect us to the greater omnipotent force. The same intelligent energy that unites to create us, our pets, our houses, Earth, and our world, creates these Spirit Helpers. An important difference to note is that these Spirit Beings are composed of higher vibrational energy and are far less dense than we are. We refer to this as subtle energy, and though the vibrations are still much higher than our own, they are more accessible than those of the very high causal level. It is because of this that they are able to bridge lower and higher energies.

We have long considered these helpers and their energies to be a part of the supernatural because we have not known what to call them or the different realms in which they "live." These Spirit Helpers exist in the energy layers of the subtle and causal that are often called the spirit or etheric realms, spirit-worlds, or the otherworlds. Quite simply, Spirit Helpers exist in the higher vibrational spiritual aspect of our everyday world.

In our contemporary culture, these Spirit Helpers are most often referred to as Spirit Guides. Spirit Guides are everywhere around us, all the time, just outside of our ordinary, everyday, five-sense perception. To those who can see and sense them, they are of a lighter form than people and things, like a semi-form, wearing a less dense cape of higher vibrational energy. These ambassadors of the great web of life are as diverse and unique as the animals and humans we see in our everyday world.

The term *Spirit Guides* is an all-encompassing term under which many different forms and types of Spirit Helpers can be defined. Depending upon culture, the form the Spirit Guides appear in, or their perceived purpose, these Spirit Helpers are commonly referred to as Guardian Spirits, Spirit Teachers, Spirit Healers, Spirit Allies, Guardian Angels, Power Animals, Totems, Gods, Goddesses, Ascended Masters, Religious Deities such as Jesus, Mother Mary, Buddha, Kuan Yin or Shiva, ancestors such as predecessors in any lineage or deceased relatives known or unknown of bloodline lineage, deceased loved ones such as friends and pets, Energies such as Christ Consciousness, Goddess Power, or Nature Guidance, or as archetypes with faces, bodies, shapes, forms, and names.

Like Spirit Guides, most of the names listed above are also broad titles used to identify a group of similar Spirit Energies. For example, the term Power Animal is not exclusive to four-legged, wild, furry land mammals, but also includes such Helping Spirits as domestic pets, birds, reptiles, amphibians, fish, insects, and water mammals. The term Ascended Masters can include Religious Deities, but also includes known and unknown masters of any discipline, such as artists, inventors, teachers, healers, saints, priests, priestesses, or shamans who were once in human form on Earth. Indeed, an infinite spectrum of powerful Spirit Masters can become available to us once we develop our awareness of them. Nature is bursting with energy and Spirit, and the term Nature Spirit or Elemental Spirit encompasses a great many different Spirit Guides. Faeries, elves, leprechauns, gnomes, the green man, forest spirit, air, fire, water, earth, plants, trees, wind, clouds, storms, sun, moon, planets, stars, and Mother Nature are powerful Spirits that are often grouped together under this term. Mythical Beings describes a category of Spirit Guides that appears in mythical form, like unicorns, pegasus, dragons, or griffins. Spirit Guides we call Angelic Beings may appear as we would typically expect an Angel to look, but they may also appear as Energy Beings without form, such as radiant, glowing orbs of light or color.

No matter the name or appearance, we all have these powerful Spirit Guides whose "job" is to guide, protect, teach, and link us with the high vibrational power of universal life-force for energy, vitality, health, and enlightenment. Guiding and teaching Spirits also strive to help us recognize our strengths, powers, and natural talents. Working with these manifestations of the web is a powerful method for energizing. To do so we need only become aware of their presence and allow ourselves to open and receive this precious high-powered gift.

Most of us have had Spirit Guides helping us throughout our lives, whether we have been consciously aware of them or not. One indicator of the presence of a Spirit Guide is having a natural attraction to or an affinity for a certain thing. Perhaps you have always loved angels, faeries, dolphins, horses, deer, wolves, eagles, unicorns, oak trees, gnomes, mountains, or a religious figure. You may have collected physical representations of them such as in books, pictures, or statues. Perhaps you are frequented by certain animals or birds in your everyday life, or you travel to areas where certain Spirits live, such as the ocean or the mountains. These are just a few examples of ways that you have already been unconsciously connected with your Spirit Guides. As you become more aware and consciously deepen your connection through guided journeys, meditations, exercises, and everyday life, they will reveal themselves to you even more.

Spirituality and Science

The existence of Spirit Guides and their assistance to those in the physical realm has been a component of every major religion and path of spirituality in human experience. Our ancestral roots and associations are steeped in this knowledge. For example, Indo-European people such as the Greeks, Celts, Romans, and Vikings spoke to gods and goddesses through oracles. Indigenous cultures globally have long called upon the power and wisdom of animals and ancestors to guide them through life, battles, and hunting. Throughout history and into modern day, Spirit Guides are as real and observable as you and me to those who employ senses such as clairvoyance (seeing), clairaudience (hearing), and clairsentience (feeling).

Some may dispute the existence of Spirit because it has not yet been scientifically measured. Fortunately, secular views are changing as cutting edge scientists and quantum physics bridge the disparities between science and spirituality. Though this is exciting, it's important not to put too much emphasis on asking science to explain the mysteries. It's extremely difficult to explain transrational concepts such as Spirit in rational terms. One of the beautiful aspects of working with Spirit is being able to experience the infinite gifts, whether we understand them scientifically or not. Transcendence is not dependent on intellect.

Native Peoples call spiritual energy The Great Mystery, and that's really what it is. We may never be able to prove or disprove the existence of the divine in energy, but with beliefs that are as universal as these, it is prudent for us to give them some consideration. Joseph Campbell teaches us that what we believe, what we are taught, what culture and time we live in, and what we search out on our own is referred to as personal mythology. Our personal mythology gives us reference, explanation, and understanding for things that happen to us and for things that happen in our world, along with faith and hope.

Like many others, my personal mythology includes the knowing that Spirit Guides are real and significant. I know they exist because I see them, feel them, sense them, and talk with them daily in my ordinary world and in my journeys, meditations, and energy connecting exercises. The energy connecting exercises that I used to heal and re-energize myself from chronic fatigue immune deficiency syndrome, fibromyalgia, asthma, and the depression that comes with these illnesses were gifts of guidance and energy from the Spirits. In fact, the journeys and exercises in this book come to you directly from Spirit Guidance.

It is futile to use the rational mind to try to dissect the mysteries of life instead of experiencing them. It is through personal experience and the felt sense that we know the truth. People who connect with the universal life-force through the divine link of our helping Spirit Guides find it to be a valid, significant, and personal experience—one that I would like to share with you. As science continues to verify what we already know from our ancestors, I invite you to sit back, take in a deep breath, and enjoy the power of the Divine Spiritual Energies, Forces, and Beings that share their potent energetic source of life with you.

A Brief Word on Spirit Protocol

The energies in the subtle and causal worlds are singularly benign and helpful. They are present to help us grow and benefit from this learning lab called Earth. They are willing to help us as much as we are willing to receive that help. We may visit them in order to get energized, but if we are open to it, they will very likely teach us things—lessons—to help us in our daily lives. Even so, sometimes their lessons can be harsh, direct, and stingingly accurate, and can leave us reeling as we process the information or experiences we have in the spirit-worlds. Lessons of this more formidable type often occur when we didn't pay attention to the soft and fuzzy ones that came first. The guidelines that follow are "the rules" that you can count on as you connect with these high vibrational energies:

1. All of the Beings, Entities, or Spirits in the subtle and causal realms are benign helping spirits that are there to benefit you. They will not possess or co-opt you in any way against your will, and they all respect and respond to the energy protections you have already learned in chapters 3 and 4. If, for any reason, you feel that there is a Spirit or Spirits that are present to harm you, *this is a product of your own pathology.* You need to address this issue as a personal one and figure out why you want to hurt yourself.

2. Spirits and Beings of higher vibration are honest and truthful and expect you to interact with them in like manner. If, over time, your motives for interacting with them are continually dishonest,

ego-oriented, or negative, they will cease to connect with and help you. They are there to give you a chance to heal and grow, not to function as vehicles for wish fulfillment or self-indulgent vanities.

3. Often, Spirit Guides will speak to you in metaphor, or dream language. Their actions are representative of the message they are trying to convey to you. Images and objects refer to what they are saying and may have no meaning by themselves. For instance, a Spirit Being may, with your permission, disassemble your energetic body, then reassemble it in order to eliminate a blockage or leakage in your field, or to let you know that you need to do your energy exercises. Maybe in the process the Being will wipe your face off and discard it in order to remove the false face that you wear in the world, so that the real and beautiful you can shine through. For years, one of my Spirit Guides would act as if he were going to eat my head. He did this in order to get me to realize that I needed to shut down my circular, habitual, and unproductive thinking.

As you begin to explore this wonderful new energetic world, just remember that you are safe, in control, and constantly benefited in your interactions with Spirit.

WHY WOULD I WANT TO CONNECT WITH DIVINE SPIRITUAL ENERGY?

The best way to understand the benefits of accessing spiritual energy is to feel, sense, see, and experience Spirit firsthand with your own felt sense.

Close your eyes, release your everyday thoughts and doings for a moment, take in a deep breath, and relax. Imagine yourself in the presence of a powerful Religious Deity, Energy, or Spirit Guide. Really feel and experience that Spiritual Being with you. Expand your mind and open all of your senses. Can you see, sense, or feel their brilliant energy glowing before you? Check in with yourself. Do you notice your senses "light up"

as you experience the high-vibrational energy that emanates from this
powerful energy?

If you can, then you understand why it is beneficial to connect regularly with an energy that is this powerful. If you had difficulty experiencing anything, relax, it's okay. It's not unusual to need a little practice in connecting. For many people it's difficult at first to surrender into the experience without guidance. The activities that follow will make spiritual energy more accessible.

. . .

Traveling to the spirit realms and inviting your Spirit Guides into your world and energy field are two sure-fire ways to increase your vibrational rate and open your personal energy field to universal life-force energy and power. The spirit realms consist of high frequency subtle and causal energy. By entering these realms, typically through altered states of consciousness, you can directly absorb this pure energy. You can also invite this energy into your ordinary world through intention, energy connecting exercises, ceremony, and ritual to awaken the realities and energy of both worlds. This is much like the energy George Lucas, writer of *Star Wars*, referred to when he referenced "the Force." "The Force" is everywhere around you and can be with you any time that you need it. If you are feeling fatigued, tired, lost, powerless, depressed, or ill, this is a signal that it is time to receive a transmission of "the Force" energy of Spirit to amplify and activate your own "Force." And when you are feeling good, this powerful energy will help you feel great!

Spirit Guides and identification with our higher powers help us to feel intimately connected in a partnership of love and respect with the energies around us. They provide a focus and a specific representation of what we are trying to access, the traits and abilities or characteristics we are attempting to embody. Energy without form is more difficult for us to understand and feel at first, whereas most people can easily feel the power and see an image in their mind of an Angel, Religious Deity, or favorite Spirit Guide.

One of our major stumbling blocks in being able to connect with higher forms of energy is our ego. Working with Spirit Guides helps us to break our ego bonds and connect with an energy and intelligence greater than our own. The ego is that part of our self that holds all the software governing our programs and behaviors that may cause energy blockages and leakages. Letting go of the ego releases these energy-draining programs. As you put effort into linking with your Spirit Guides, you slowly begin to step outside of yourself and your problems and identify with the vast world of Spirit and energy. This expanded global focus slowly erodes the limitations of the ego and opens up your energy field to the infinite energies of the universe. By allowing the Spirits to help you bridge from your denser energy to their lighter, higher vibrational rate, you are able to piggyback on their power to overcome any ego-created energy loss, doubt, and feeling of powerlessness. Every time you achieve this you increase your own vibrational level and sense of self-power. With this added power your essence expands to give you the energy that you need to find passion and joy in life, to have direction and purpose, and to live, rather than merely exist.

Connecting with spiritual energy has many additional benefits beyond giving you direct access to high vibrational energy for energizing yourself. Spiritual energy is conscious and intelligent and can be accessed for such things as guidance, wisdom, knowledge, healing, improving quality of life, and creating miracles. This is not to say that it is a panacea to save us from life's struggles, but rather it adds a very powerful tool to our toolbox of activities for responding with strength and poise to life's challenges. During a recent spiritual training I attended, someone likened the relationship between Spirit Guides and humans to the analogy of a sporting event. They are in the stands cheering us on and coaching us from the sidelines, while we are on the playing field dealing with the skirmishes. This image should remind us that we are in charge of our life, but we don't have to do it all alone. When we stand firmly in our power, ask for assistance from the other realms, and engage something more than our ordinary world, we are able to manifest energy, abundance, and miracles.

How to Connect with Divine Spiritual Energy

In the past, shamans, priestesses, and priests were the wisdom keepers and teachers whose job it was to bridge the ordinary physical world with the nonordinary world of the Spirits for health, balance, harmony, and guidance. We can all benefit here and now by bridging the wisdom and power of the Spirits to heal and energize ourselves and our stressful world. We all have the innate ability; we need only to retrain ourselves to effectively access the unseen.

As children we all came into this world with a special gift. We had a natural spirituality, a magical creative part of our self that saw and believed in Spirit Guides and the otherworlds. Can you remember? Before you were trained to think with your left brain so you could fit into a rational, egocentric, technological, contemporary world, your mystical experiences were real and potent. The childlike innocence and openness that allowed you to be receptive and perceptive to Spirit back then is your ticket back to connection with the powers of the spiritual nonordinary. If you need energy, then it is time for you to reclaim your inherent magical mysticism. As you practice the energy connecting activities that follow in this chapter, allow the imaginative, curious child inside of you to come out and play.

You can connect with Divine Spiritual Energy in all the same ways that you have learned to connect with universal life-force energy because the two are essentially one and the same. In order to see, sense, feel, connect with, and utilize divine life-force energy you must become open, perceptive, and receptive. Once you have made contact with and know who your personal Spirit Guides are, you can also call upon them directly by practicing prayer, ritual, ceremony, or invocation, or simply asking them to connect with you. These are all accomplished through intention, focus, openness, and mindfulness.

Mindfulness is bare awareness in the present moment. In the singular silence of the present moment there is no past or future. A still mind, without the whirl of churning thoughts, anchors the heart in the present and opens the path to clear vision. Clear vision facilitates self-knowledge, relaxation, inner peace, and joy, and opens the gateway to connecting with Spirit Guides and the high-vibrational subtle and causal energies of the spirit-worlds.

A specific activity of mindful awareness that helps us become open to the urgings of Spirit in the ordinary world is Omenology. By paying attention to and interpreting the things that happen around us, we can become conscious of the internal and universal messages and signposts that mark our paths through life. These messages are available everywhere within ourselves and our worlds when we look, listen, feel, and acknowledge. If we use our native intuition to let the significance of those occurrences blossom within us, they will give us insight and guidance. We will also then begin to notice synchronicities and uncanny events that seem ironic, such as a long-lost friend calling just as your mind has drifted to thinking about him or her. These synchronicities are ways that our Spirit Guides make contact with us to get our attention and bestow guidance, energy, and teaching.

Often when we don't honor these messages, Spirit takes matters into its own hands, and the omens appear to us to teach us lessons. For example, while attending a spiritual training workshop in the Pocono Mountains of northern Pennsylvania, I had the opportunity to go for a run on the Appalachian Trail. I knew prior to this run that I was in deep need of grounding, but this being the first time I had been to the Appalachian Trail, I was eager to run there. I headed out without taking time for my morning energy connecting rituals, which include Earth-energy grounding. Bounding down the trail, happy as a lark, my foot caught a stone, and I ended up sprawled on the ground on my belly. At the exact moment of my fall, a crow flew over cawing. I laughed and yelled back, "Yes, I know! I needed grounding." And there I lay, hugging the mountain until my body was full. My reminder to pay attention was a swollen, jammed middle finger. I remembered that omen for a while!

Another way to connect with Spirit and to energize yourself is by creating an altar. An altar establishes a sacred space that is directly linked to your Spirit Guides and the universal life-force. "Hearth is the place where the universe comes together," teaches Tom Cowan, a shaman and author in the Celtic tradition. An altar consists of physical representations and symbols of Spirit energy and power that resonate and nurture your soul; therefore, whatever you put on your altar and however you set up your altar is correct for you. Ideas of things to place on your altar are pictures, statues, ornaments, necklaces, stones, crystals, candles, plants, seeds, flowers, incense, and water—anything that connects you with Spirit. Pictures and statues on altars often represent Deities, Power Animals, and Spirit Guides that work with you. Candles, water, incense, and stones can represent the elements of fire, water, air, and earth, respectively, but may also be objects of special power that were given to you by Spirit Guides or were used in ritual or celebration. Crystals, plants, seeds, and flowers bring in the Spirits of nature to your sacred space, and these, too, can come from special places or events to hold the power of that place accessible to you.

An altar can be set up anywhere, inside or out, but if you can, try to find an out-of-the-way space to set up your objects of power so that others won't disturb them. Use any design that suits you, and be creative and dynamic. To keep energy flowing, bring in new energies and objects as you see fit. Spend time with your altar daily if you can, even if only to quickly acknowledge each Spirit represented there. In this way, you continually stay energized by connecting to your Spirit Guides, the Spirits of the elements and nature, and the universal life-force energy that runs through the great web of life.

As in the last chapter, the following guided journey, meditation, and exercises will help you hone your skills of sensing, perceiving, and receiving universal life-force energy in its spiritual form by employing the five-step process of intention, focus, releasing, allowing, and accepting.

GUIDED JOURNEY

Connect with Energy by Meeting Your Spirit Guides

Go to a soft space where you will not be disturbed, and turn off all telephones. If indoors, dim the lights and play relaxing music, if you'd like. Sit or lie down where you will feel warm and comfortable, safe and protected. Take a moment to quiet yourself. Take in a deep breath and relax. Allow your eyes to naturally close. Take a few moments to cleanse your energy field by using the Rainbow Waterfall exercise. After several moments of clearing, allow yourself to soften into deep relaxation using the Universal Induction.

As you continue to relax, imagine that you are walking down a path in the woods, feeling light, and connected with nature. It's a beautiful day, filled with soft sunlight and a warm, gentle breeze. A slow and easy, perfect day. Use all of your senses to feel the universal life-force energy, and enjoy your connection with Mother Earth. As you stroll down this path in the woods, you notice any birds that flit back and forth from tree to tree. Breathe deeply of the fresh, forested air. Slowly, as you stroll along the path, the woods open up into a heavenly meadow filled with wildflowers of all colors. You notice the bees and the butterflies as they flit and float from flower to flower, paying you no mind. You slowly meander through this heavenly meadow, feeling calm and connected with Mother Nature. Use all of your senses to feel the universal life-force energy. As you continue to stroll down this path through the beautiful meadow, the path leads to a vivid rainbow that climbs high into the sky. Step inside the rainbow, and experience the power and beauty of the radiant colors.

Lifting you up with its magical powers, the rainbow converts into a moving bridge that transports you up into the Spirit world. Higher and higher you ascend through the sky until you reach a cloud mass, outside of time and space. On the other side of the soft, billowy clouds, a crystal castle with exquisite gardens and lush, green grounds shimmers in the distance. Intrigued, you exit the rainbow bridge and begin to explore this wondrous place by strolling through the lush, green grounds. You notice that you are naturally using all of your senses to experience everything that you see, sense, and feel on your journey.

While exploring the grounds, you become aware of an animal approaching you. The animal is friendly, and it feels safe and familiar, even though you may not have ever met this animal before. The animal comes near you, your eyes meet, and it mentally communicates a message to you that it is your Power Animal. You reach out and touch the animal, feeling the texture of its body and sensing its powerful energy. The next few moments you spend getting to know one another and sharing energy.

Drawn by the magic of the gardens and the sparkling castle, you and your Power Animal cross the grounds and enter one of the gardens. It is filled with vibrant, colored flowers, and their fragrant scents fill your senses immediately. Your Power Animal playfully nudges one of the flowers, and a Nature Sprite flies out of the center, sputtering at the grinning animal. You chuckle at the interchange and quickly introduce yourself to the Sprite before it disappears back into the flower. Startled by the sound of flapping wings, you look up to see a bird swoop down into the garden and land on the ornamental tree before you.

Similar to when you met your Power Animal, the bird is friendly, and it feels safe and familiar, even though you may not have ever met this bird before. The bird cocks its head, your eyes meet, and it mentally communicates a message to you that it, too, is one of your Spirit Guides. Your Power Animal nods in agreement. You reach out and touch the bird, feeling the texture of its feathers and sensing its powerful energy. The next few moments you spend getting to know one another and sharing energy.

The castle sparkles in the sunlight, catching your eye and inviting you to come closer. Standing beneath its towering presence, you are in awe of its magnificent beauty and power. You enter the castle and take your time exploring the many rooms.

Tucked away in a hidden corner, you discover a round room that looks like a crystal cave. The curved walls and domed ceiling sparkle with the brilliant energies and colors of every crystal imaginable. Warm and inviting, the room contains two large plush chairs and many soft, fluffy pillows and blankets. Seated in one of the chairs is a Spirit Being, who invites you to come and sit with it.

Similar to when you met your Power Animal, the Spirit is friendly and feels safe and familiar, even though you may not have ever met this Spirit before. Your eyes meet, and the Spirit reassuringly tells you that it, too, is one of your Spirit Guides. You know in your heart that this is true. Your Spirit Guide opens its energy field to you and allows you to sense its powerful energy. You feel the energy and notice how your energy responds. The next few moments you spend getting to know one another and sharing energy.

With open energy boundaries, you allow the powerful energy of your Spirit Guide to soak into your body and soul. Relax and feel the strength and the power of your Spirit Guide filling you with the potent energy of the universal life-force. Feel this energy connecting with and stimulating your own personal energy. Feel power and vibrancy returning to your body and soul. Experience yourself filled with the high-vibrational energy of Spirit. Every cell of your body is saturated with this glowing, healing, revitalizing energy.

At the prompting of your Spirit Guide, you ask for a personal teaching, some words of guidance or wisdom, and you open your mind and soul to receive the gift with your heart. Your body, mind, emotions, and soul are enveloped in pure harmony and balance.

Take in a deep breath, and allow this energy to deepen within your body and soul. Feel the vibrations growing stronger and stronger within you, with every breath that you take, and every beat of your heart. With each passing moment, your essence absorbs the life-force energy, and you grow profoundly.

When you are ready to return, gratefully thank your Spirit Guide for its presence, help, and energy. You mentally rise from your special spot and leave the castle, walking slowly through the beautiful gardens with your bird and animal Spirit Guides. Breathing deeply of all the powerful life-force energy, as you reach the rainbow bridge, you turn to look once more into the beautiful gardens and say goodbye to your Spirit Guide friends. Gathering one last deep breath of this healing, calm, peaceful *power, you step onto the rainbow bridge and begin to descend back into your soft space and your body as you count back from the number ten to one. With every number you become more awake and more alert, being fully awake and alert at the number one. Ten, begin descending the rainbow bridge; nine, eight, seven, six, going down; five, four, three, becoming more awake; two, one, back in your body, fully awake and alert, and feeling better than you have in a long, long time.*

Sit quietly for a few moments and reflect on your experience. Be gentle with yourself as you wiggle and stretch, becoming fully present in your body and conscious mind. Express your experience, thoughts, and feelings in your journal.

MEDITATION

Connect with Di vine Spiritual Energy

Sit in quiet contemplation in your nature place or in a soft space where you will not be disturbed. Open your mind and relax. Observe, notice, and feel everything that you experience. Focus your attention on your feelings, and open up all of your senses to experience your meditation. Allow any distracting thoughts to drift away. Notice them and let them go.

Sit quietly and observe yourself. See, sense, feel, and experience everything about yourself, inside and out. Ask Spirit to come and be with you. If you know who your Spirit Guides are, invite them to come and sit with you. If you worship or work with certain Religious Deities, ask them to come and sit with you. What do you see, sense, or feel? Who or what is the Spirit Energy that is with you? Does it have a form or a body? Does it give you a sense or a feeling? Notice its attributes and characteristics. Is there any light emanating from it? Is there more than one? What colors do you see? Sense and feel their energy. Sense and feel your own energy. What do you feel physically? What do you feel emotionally? What do you sense inside of your body? Is there any energy movement? What do you sense outside of your body? Is there any energy movement? Sometimes Spirit works with the elements. Do you notice any elements? Do any of the elements blend together? Relax, look deeper, and continue to observe for a while. Allow yourself to sense and feel everything about the Spirit Energies around you, and the empty space in between. Allow yourself to sense and feel all of your thoughts and the empty space in between. Allow yourself to sense and feel all of your emotions and the empty space in between. Allow yourself to sense and feel the physical energy of your body and the empty space in between. Sense and feel the energy that is all four, and the space in between. Breathe deeply of this energy. Notice your sensations.

Now close your eyes. Allow the power of the Spirit Energies and your inner wisdom to bubble forth. Relax, focus, and feel. Open up to feeling all of the energy moving around and through you. Allow questions and answers to form in and out of your thoughts. Questions like: Do the Spirit Energies affect my energy levels? Do the Spirit Energies affect my chakras? Are they open and spinning? What am I feeling in the chakra locations? Do I feel energy moving around and through me? Do the Spirit Energies affect the different layers of my energy field? Can I feel these? Can I see these? What colors do I see, feel, or sense? What vibrations do I see, feel, or sense? What messages do the Spirit Energies have to share with me? Is there any wisdom that the Spirit Energies would like to share with me? If so, what? What healing energies do the Spirit Energies have to share with me?

Stay in this place in contemplation for as long as you have time, asking your own questions of yourself. When you are ready, take in a deep breath and allow yourself a few moments to shift your awareness back to ordinary life and fully integrate back into your body. Write your thoughts and feelings in your journal.

EXERCISES TO CONNECT WITH SPIRITUAL ENERGY

Luminous spiritual energy is everywhere around you all the time. All you need to do to access it is to open your mind, become aware, and willfully make a connection. The imaginative mystical part of yourself that craves to connect with Spirit will love the following exercises which can be performed anywhere at any time since you do not need to enter into an altered state of consciousness for them to be effective. Practice these exercises as they are, or, if you have the time and are in an appropriate place, you may choose to enter into an altered state of consciousness, as described in chapter one, for added relaxation and receptivity.

Meet with Your Spirit Guides

This exercise to meet with your Spirit Guides is similar to the guided journey above, minus the process of entering into an altered state of consciousness and traveling to the Spirit Guide. In this exercise you will invite your Spirit Guide to come and meet with you wherever you are at that moment. You can connect with Spirit Guides anytime, anywhere, simply by becoming open and aware, and inviting Spirit Energies to come and be with you. This exercise will give you some experience in opening this doorway.

Begin by taking in a deep breath, relaxing, and closing your eyes. Let go of your everyday thoughts and concerns. Feel your mind quiet and your whole self become calm and peaceful. When you feel relaxed, invite a Spirit Guide to come and sit with you. Be open and receptive to who or whatever appears. Use all of your senses to experience the presence of your Spirit Guide. You may not be able to "see" it at first, so notice what you are feeling, sensing, and experiencing. When your Spirit Guide arrives, ask for a personal teaching—some words of guidance, wisdom, or a healing. Open your mind and soul, and receive this gift with your heart. Ask for an energy exchange. Feel the high-vibrational energy that comprises your Spirit Guide. Notice how your energy feels being in the

presence of its energy. See, sense, feel, and experience all of the ways that
your energy field changes by being in the presence of your Spirit Guide. Ask
your Guide to let you see its energy so that you can recognize its energy,
aspects, nuances, patterns, vibrations, sound, color, and what form it
takes, if any. Ask your Guide to tell you about its energetic qualities and
attributes. Listen with your heart. Don't worry if it feels like you are mak-
ing it up; it often feels that way at first. Remain open and accepting of
whatever comes to you.

When you are finished with the exercise, thank your Spirit Guide for sharing its presence and energy with you. Maintain the energy flow as you go about your daily life.

Connecting with Nature and Earth Elemental Spirit Beings

The Connecting with Nature and Earth Elemental Spirit Beings exercise will help you to recognize the Spirit-that-moves-in-all-things. The web of life is all things, and all things are a part of the great web. All things have a spirit and are made of energy. In this exercise our intention is to connect with the powerful energies of nature and the elements. The list of Nature Spirits and Earth Elementals is endless, and includes such Beings as Nature Sprites, faeries, divas, gnomes, elves, plant spirits, crystal spirits, rock spirits, tree spirits, fire spirits, water spirits, air spirits, clouds, Mother Nature, the forest spirit, and the green man, to name just a few. These Spirits have been ignored by mankind for a long time, so be patient as you attempt to connect with them. It may take them a little while to trust you.

Go to a place in nature or a place of nature in your mind. Close your
eyes, take in a deep breath, and relax. Open your mind and activate all of
your senses. Let go of your everyday thoughts and concerns. Feel your
mind quiet and your whole self become calm and peaceful. When you feel
relaxed, invite a Nature Spirit to come and be with you. Be open and

receptive to who or whatever appears. Use all of your senses to experience
the presence of the Spirit. You may not be able to "see" it at first, so notice
what you are feeling, sensing, and experiencing. The key to connecting is
to open your mind and soul. Feel the quality and intensity of the energy
that comprises it. Notice how your energy feels being in the presence of its
energy. See, sense, feel, and experience all the ways that your energy field
changes by being in its presence. Ask it to let you see its energy so that you
can recognize its energy, aspects, nuances, patterns, vibrations, sound,
color, and what form it takes, if any. Ask it to tell you about its energetic
qualities and attributes. Listen with your heart, and be respectful.

When you are finished with the exercise, thank the Spirits who visited
you for sharing their presence and energy with you. Maintain the
energy flow as you go about your daily life.

Omen Reading

Omen Reading isn't an exercise that you do like the others; it is mindful
awareness that you practice during your busy everyday life. Through
omens, Spirit sends you guidance, wisdom, healing, and energy to keep
you energized and alert to possible energy leakage and blockage situations that you can correct on the spot. Spirit is always sending you
energy and speaking to you; you need only be open and pay attention to
perceive, receive, hear, see, and read the energy and messages that come
to you as omens. Energy and messages are easily noticed and recogniz-
able when you are awake, aware, and alert to the things that happen to
you and around you. Let's practice.

Close your eyes, take in a deep breath, and relax. Let go of all thoughts
about your worldly concerns. Think about something that you noticed
recently during your everyday life that sticks in your mind as a possible
omen. Perhaps you saw a hawk swoop down in your yard or the image of

a red knight on a truck in front of you, or maybe you heard a significant song on the radio. Whatever it was, notice how it makes you feel right now as you think about it. What else do you notice? What are you thinking, sensing, experiencing? What kind of message and energy does this omen bring to you? Allow it to sink into your mind, body, and energy field. Experience the energy for as long as you have time.

In a similar manner to this practice exercise, you can open up your awareness, energy field, body, and mind to sense, experience, and understand the energies and meanings of omens as they occur throughout your day.

Altar Connection

In the Altar Connection exercise, you are connecting with Spirit Energies through the altar that you have created as described earlier in this chapter. If you haven't created your altar yet, begin by doing that. When your altar is finished, you will always have a place that has been established as sacred space.

Sit before your altar, then light a candle and some incense or sage if you'd like. Put on some soft meditative music or rattle lightly, take in a deep breath, and relax. Ease your conscious mind into a state of gratitude and reverence. Place your hands in prayer position at your chest, and bow before the Spirit Energies represented on the altar in respect and honor. Ask your Spirit Guides to come and join you in your sacred space. Open your mind and your energy field to experience their presence. Feel the frequency of the energy that comprises them. Notice how your energy feels being in the presence of their energy.

When you are finished with the exercise, thank the Spirits who visited you for sharing their presence and energy with you. Maintain the energy flow as you go about your daily life.

Filling with Spiritual Power

The Filling with Spiritual Power exercise entails inviting Spirit to be present inside of your body and energy field. This directly connects you to Spirit and energizes you with the high-vibrational energies they emanate. By inviting the Spirit Guide or Spirit Form of your choice into your body and energy field, you will stimulate your energy field to vibrate at their frequency. This is incredibly energizing and enlightening.

Begin by taking in a deep breath, closing your eyes, and relaxing for a moment. If you have time, clear yourself of blockages and unwanted energy by using your favorite exercise from chapter three. When you are ready, mindfully bring your awareness to your center and go deep within to your inner self. Ask a Spirit Guide, Religious Deity, or Spirit Form to join you. Acknowledge its presence. See, sense, and feel it standing before you. Be aware and use all of your senses to experience the Spirit Guide with you. Notice all of its attributes: its shape, size, color, characteristics, and so on.

Ask the Spirit Guide if it would step inside your energy field so that you can experience its energy. See, sense, and feel it standing directly in front of you, lined up chakra to chakra. When you feel yourselves fully lined up, allow the merging to take place. Open up your energy boundary with your intention, and feel the Guide step into your energy field. See, sense, and feel its energies blending with you. Sit quietly and feel its presence and power. Experience yourself filling with dynamic high frequency energy. See, sense, feel, experience, and receive for as long as you have time.

When you are ready to disengage, thank your Spirit Guide and feel it totally separating from you as it steps out of your energy field. Remain silent for a few moments, and notice everything that you sense and feel. Do you find that you can still feel the powerful energetic signature left behind by the energy of the Spirit Guide? Feel the increase in your energy, and maintain that energy flow as you go about your daily life.

Blending with Spirit

The Blending with Spirit exercise is a powerful tradition practiced the world over throughout history by every spiritual or religious practice known. Christians call it the Jesus Prayer and Filling with the Holy Spirit, Buddhists call it Putting on the Cloak or Mind of Buddha, Sufis call it Welcoming the Friend, Shamans call it Merging and Shape-Shifting, and Esotericists call it the Assumption of the God Form.

This exercise is similar to the Filling with Spiritual Power exercise, but with a different twist. In the Filling with Spiritual Power exercise you are inviting Spirit to come into your energy field. However, in this exercise you are stepping into the energy field of the Spirit Guide of your choice and feeling its high-vibrational energy. This exercise will undeniably raise your vibrations and energy levels. If you are interested in spiritual growth and enlightenment, this exercise will also help you progress along your path by allowing you to directly experience the higher vibrational energies of Spirit.

Choose a Spirit Guide, Religious Deity, or Spirit Form that you would like to merge with energetically. Take in a deep breath and relax. Study a picture or object representation of the Spirit Guide that you have chosen for this exercise. If you don't have one, or prefer to connect through your own image, close your eyes and picture the Spirit Form as tangibly as possible in your mind's eye. Invite the Spirit Guide to come and stand before you. Notice all of its attributes: its shape, size, color, posture, garments, characteristics, and so on.

Close your eyes, and in your mind's eye, see, sense, and feel an image of the Spirit in front of you. Use all of your senses to really manifest its presence by seeing it, sensing it, and feeling it. It should be huge and towering before you. Amplify all of the particulars of the Spirit Guide. Notice all of its attributes: its shape, size, color, posture, garments, characteristics, and so on. The energy should be palpable with your felt sense.

Ask the Spirit Guide permission to enter its energy field, and when permission is granted, take one step forward and enter the Spirit Guide.

Inhabit the Spirit Guide completely. Speak the name or the form of the Spirit Guide out loud, and feel the vibration of the sound. Repeat three times while you see, sense, and feel yourself enclosed in the energy field of the Spirit Guide. Sense yourself fully blended with the Spirit Guide. Assume its stance, posture, expression, and any other nuance about it you can discern. Allow yourself to feel its energy, to be its energy, and to feel what it is like to be that Spirit Guide. Relax and take your time. Allow yourself to feel its consciousness and to be its consciousness. Completely merge and blend energetically with the Spirit Guide. Allow it to feel your energy and consciousness. As completely as possible, be that Spirit Guide.

When you are ready to disengage, take one step backward and separate yourself from the Spirit Guide. See and feel yourself as a separate entity. See the Spirit Guide towering before you and then slowly disappearing.

Remain silent for a few moments, and notice everything that you sense and feel. Do you find that you can still feel the powerful energetic signature left behind by the energy of the Spirit Guide? Maintain this energy flow as you go about your daily life.

• • •

Now that you have begun to experience how to blend the high vibrations of Divine Spiritual Energy and universal life-force power with your own energy, your aura is most likely radiating with a joyful brilliant glow that outshines the "old you" that used to struggle to get through the day. To delve even deeper into the mysteries of self and energy, the next chapter will introduce you to concepts and activities that will help you return to pure source energy.

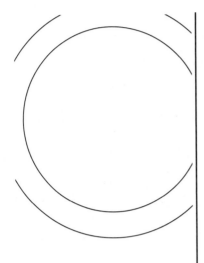

SEVEN

Return to Source

You can be God,
or you can be an ego
pretending to be God.
It's your choice.
~Ken Wilber, Boomeritis

Brilliant, lively, universal life-force energy is within you and everywhere around you in every single moment, sustaining your body, energy field, family, home, friends, community, world, universe, and cosmos. Through the guided journeys, meditations, and energy connecting exercises, you have experienced this energy firsthand, and perhaps you have had some inspiring experiences connecting with your personal energy, universal life-force energy, and the divine.

As a result, you have experienced that you are much more than a bag of flesh with a brain that allows you to have conscious thoughts and emotions. By activating your energy field you have felt the energizing power and strength of the dynamic force that sustains your life and makes you an energy being—a Spirit similar to your Spirit Guides—living in a human body. Your personal energy forms a natural link to the higher vibrational energies of the universe that exist everywhere. You have already experienced this by connecting with and embodying the universal life-force and Spirit energies.

Thus far, the energy that you have experienced has been from a closed internal and an open external system perspective. Chapters two through four helped you stimulate your energy field, release blockages, and stop leakages in your closed energy system. In chapters five and six you opened up your energy system to connect with and embody the energies of the universal life-force and the divine. The energy that is generated by your body and energy system seems to originate from an internal source, while the energies of the universal life-force and Spirit seem to come from external sources. Though these energies seem to be different and to originate from different places, they all originate from the same intelligent source.

As you recall from chapters 1 and 5, undifferentiated universal life-force energy is the first manifestation of the potential of the cosmos. Over time, bits of this undifferentiated universal life-force energy slowly coalesced into the causal energies and myriad subtle energies until some of it finally settled into the many forms of dense matter we see today in the physical world. In a very real sense, everything that is, is universal life-force energy. Even so, the permeating background sea of undifferentiated universal life-force energy is still present at each moment everywhere in our physical universe and in the subtle and causal realms, or spirit-worlds. It is the driving force of intelligence, life, and creation in this and every world.

Because the term undifferentiated universal life-force energy is such a mouthful, I will refer to it as "source" energy, or as the "source." It is important to remember that source energy precedes all later forms of universal life-force energy. It is the formless precursor to everything, and can be thought of as pregnant, hyperenergized, pure void.

Because everything we can observe, including ourselves, is made up of densified universal life-force energy, and because this energy proceeds from and floats in the source, everything has a fundamental access to source energy. Everything has a back door, if you will, that makes it possible for the formless source to be experienced. This makes it possible for us to experience source energy through a variety of activities. We can pass through to the void of source via space, nature, our inner selves, or even our Spirit Guides or the spirit-worlds.

The great advantage of dissolving into the formless void is that it allows us to shed the shackles and chains of our physical bodies and minds. In the place of emptiness before thought can arise, we are able to float completely in a singular moment outside of time and space within an energy that connects everything.

Because source energy is infinitely alive, intelligent, and omnipresent, it resembles many traditional concepts of God. Differentiating source energy from our spiritual and religious beliefs is impossible and irrelevant, so I encourage you to decide based on your own orientation, teachings, and personal mythology if the energy that you will be blending with is causal energy, source energy, or an energy that is spiritual, divine, or Godly. Also based on your beliefs, I recommend that you add whatever terms or names to my designations of source energy that will help you unite with this energy.

Whether you believe in the divine or not, whether you follow a specific religion or not, source energy affects you both internally and externally. It is oneness with this energy that is your "Godliness" and the web of life that your soul and energy field yearn to be connected with at all times. In your natural state, you are not separate from this great energy;

you are fully immersed in it and are made of it. It is only in disconnection that separation exists, and when you are separate from this energy, you are out of harmony and balance. When you can release yourself and become it, you are no longer separate from the oneness of the great web of life. Harmony, balance, transcendence from the ordinary, and unlimited energy are the gifts that can then settle into your everyday life.

WHAT IS RETURNING TO SOURCE?

Returning to source is a conscious blending of both the closed and open energy systems that you have experienced by dissolving form and barriers. It is a technique that yields powerful benefits. The only thing preventing you from relating intimately with this energy is the illusion that you are somehow different and separate from it. The same energy source that creates and animates you creates and animates everything. Therefore, in the grander scheme of things, you are not energetically separate from other things, people, places, Spirit Beings, or the universal life-force energies that give you life. Energetically, you are already one with source; you need only shift your perspective to understand and experience the powerful energy in this inherent union.

Why Is Returning to Source Helpful?

Blending with the abundant, free-flowing, high vibrational, pure life-force of source energy is like raising your personal energy voltage from 110 to 220. This life-sustaining energy will give you a boost of energy that will vastly increase your vitality and vibrancy.

Becoming source energy invites healing to every level of your being. Your energy field will be stimulated, your soul nurtured, every cell of your body therapeutically bathed in a sea of loving energy, your mind centered and calm, and your emotions balanced. By bringing your physical, spiritual, mental, and emotional focus together into the present moment, this activity changes your ordinary world awareness into one of higher consciousness. This, coupled with high frequency energy, creates a powerful remedy for many physical illnesses and mental or emotional hurdles like depression and anxiety.

Modern doctors and psychologists subscribe to the concept that physical, mental, and emotional problems are caused by biological and environmental factors. In most cases I agree, but would add that often the biological or environmental factors are a result of, or are exacerbated by, energy deficiencies. For example, anxiety occurs when we feel disconnected, feel out of control, and are not in the present moment. Circular thoughts of the past or anticipation of the future take you out of the present moment. This creates energy loss. Physical, mental, and emotional problems are also the by-products of energy loss that is the result of separation from source energy. Returning to source brings you back into the present moment, transforms you into energy by releasing your form and separateness, and brings calm and balance back into your life. In a simple and nurturing way, in fifteen minutes or less, you have energetically circumvented the culprits that cause energy drain.

One of the most beautiful aspects of becoming source energy is the innate sense of oneness and belonging that seeps into your consciousness and everyday life. The experience of unity that comes from becoming source energy will energize and empower you with omnipotent universal support and strength. This can powerfully eradicate feelings of isolation and disconnection. When you are pure source energy you are not a separate being—you are one with everything—and this creates balance and harmony in your body and soul that brings an innate sense of peace and calmness. Once you experience and practice this, it becomes easy to blend the creative energies of the universe outside and inside of yourself to energize you and your life. For some, this is a small miracle, and miracles are what this creative energy force is all about.

The same source energy that created the world can give you the power to help you manifest wonderful things, abundant energy, and miracles in your life. It can also help to bring about change, peace, and miracles in the world. Source energy has an intelligence that reflects intentional thoughts and emotions. By using mental focus and strong intention, you can create a more harmonious life and world. Imagine what it would be like if millions of people collectively motivated source energy to create and manifest a world full of energy, health, love, and peace for all. It is this very concept and energy that my teacher, author Sandra Ingerman, is using to transmute toxins and pollution in people and the earth through her teachings and book *Medicine for the Earth*. If you have an interest in healing the Earth and changing the world, this book comes highly recommended.

How to Return to Source

Returning to source is returning to your own formless essence, the pure high-frequency energy that is you. Because you are already well-versed in connecting with universal and spiritual energies that seem to be "external," it may be easiest to return to source by first experiencing "external" source energy and then blending with it. The act of becoming, blending, and uniting with energy is different from connecting with or embodying energy. To return to source is to be energy in complete union with energy. In this process the self acts as a distant observer experiencing the evaporation of itself and its form into pure energy. It is a simple process of shifting your focus from your physical world to your energetic world by allowing your mind, emotions, and physical form to dissolve, envisioning the source energy that created you as the source energy within you, and using your felt sense to experience this.

The first step in returning to source is a conscious release of the illusion that you are separate from source energy. The illusion of separation comes from the ego and our perception of duality. The ego is the part of our psyche that defines self and acts as the mediator between the self and the rest of the world. Our perception of duality comes from living in a world that is full of dual opposites like light and dark, good and bad, science and spirituality, republican and democrat, and so on.

Underneath these obvious examples of duality lies the real cause of energy loss. Duality gives us a "me versus them" perception, a feeling that we are separate from everything and fundamentally in opposition with it. To become your true essence you need to let go of the worldly concerns and attachments that keep you bound to the physical, materialistic, dualistic world, and separate from source. This entails shifting your focus from your physical world to your energetic world by allowing your mind, emotions, and physical form to dissolve. It is a simple step, and yet a difficult one at first for some. It is amazing how attached to our physical world we can be.

Once you have shifted your focus away from your self and your everyday world, the next step can be accomplished in several ways. One way is to travel from where you are to an "outer external source," like to your soft space, a place in nature, the core of the Earth, the cosmos, the universe, heaven, or the void. Another way is to travel within your own soul and energy field to your "inner spring" of source energy. Yet another way is to stay wherever you are and blend with the source energy inherent in that place or in an "external" object such as a crystal, a tree, a mountain, or the stars.

No matter which "place" you choose, the technique is the same. Take in a deep breath, relax, and focus your attention on the present moment. Using all of your senses, experience the source energy that is present in this place. Take in a few deep breaths, and on your next inhalation intentionally draw in the source energy. See, sense, and feel the energy resonate with the same energy that lives within you. After a few moments, dissolve your form, the physical body, and self that you think you are, and allow yourself to experience yourself as source energy.

If you choose to blend with an object, be thoughtful and considerate. The object that you have chosen is a living, sentient being, and blending with it without asking permission is an unethical and disrespectful invasion. Center yourself, and ask permission of the object to blend with the source energy contained within it. Stay present in the moment and aware of yourself and the consciousness of the object. Allow yourself to experience the answer with your senses. If the answer is yes, you can blend by either sending your energy into the energy field of the object or by inviting its energy into your energy field. In either case, you then dissolve yourself by first sensing the life-force energy in the object, then melting further into the source energy from which it springs.

The following guided journey, meditation, and exercises will help you return to source using your skills of intention, focus, releasing, allowing, and accepting. The guided journey will take you into the source energy of the void. This void is an external and an internal "place" where source energy is all that exists. There are no forms—nothing but pure high vibrational energy. People who travel to the void have differing experiences. Some see nothingness, some see fullness, some see darkness, some see bright light, and others see darkness sparkling with light within it. People experience the void as nothing and everything, pregnant with creative potential and dynamic energy.

GUIDED JOURNEY

Return to Source: External Void

Go to a soft space where you will not be disturbed, and turn off all telephones. If indoors, dim the lights and play relaxing music, if you'd like. Sit or lie down where you will feel warm and comfortable, safe and protected. Take a moment to quiet yourself. Take in a deep breath and relax. Allow your eyes to naturally close. Take a few moments to cleanse your energy field by using the Rainbow Waterfall exercise. After several moments of clearing, allow yourself to soften into deep relaxation by using the Universal Induction.

Remaining completely relaxed, begin to prepare yourself for your trip out into the great void. Using the power of your mind, travel to a space center. Imagine yourself stepping onto an automated platform and riding up the side of the rocket that will carry you into space. Hoisting yourself over onto the nose, you slip into a seat that fits you just perfectly. You click your seat belt and grab hold of the handles with excited anticipation as the engines roar. "Five, four, three, two, one, and we have liftoff," you hear over the loudspeakers. Though this may not be a typical activity for you, you know that you are safe, so you let yourself relax into the feeling of exhilaration. Blasting through the sky, you feel the wind caressing your face and flowing through your hair. Climbing higher and higher, you rocket through the Earth's atmosphere into the universe. You pass by the moon, several planets, and millions upon millions of stars pulsating with energy and light on your way into the deep outermost cosmos. Leaving behind the world as you know it, you enter into the great void. No longer needed, the rocket dissolves and you find yourself gently floating in the vastness of the void.

Suspended in what appears to be nothingness, you are aware that the void is infinite and boundless. Your senses scan the amazing vastness that created the big bang and life, and your mind ponders how this could have occurred in this place that seems to be empty. You notice that there are no forms here, yet in this seemingly barren place beyond outer space there is a sensation of fullness that begins to penetrate your awareness. Opening your senses further, you become cognizant of an invisible energy, the pure high vibrational force that is source energy. It is everywhere and yet nowhere. You can feel it around you and throughout the vastness of the void. You feel it moving through you, entering on your breath, and swirling through your body and energy field. Feeling its energizing powers awaken your senses even more, you utilize this openness to further experience the aspects and characteristics of the void.

People's experiences of the void differ, so you take a few moments to notice what it is like for you. You notice if it is dark, or light. If it's dark, you notice if the darkness is a deep darkness or a soft darkness. If it's light, you notice if it is a bright light or a gentle light. You notice if it is a velvety darkness teeming with tiny twinkling lights, or a soft light filled with minute dark spots. You are aware of everything that you see, smell, taste, feel, sense, and experience.

The creative potential of the source energy is palpable, and you simultaneously sense the nothingness and the everythingness. Your mind slips into consideration of the words that we use to describe source energy, like the divine, the one, the source, the truth, the light, pure love, Godliness, and so on. You notice how each of these names resonates for you, and how each of these names resonates with the energy of the void. You know that there is no right or wrong, so you just relax and experience whatever it is that you are experiencing.

When you are ready, your awareness turns inward, and you notice yourself as a part of the void. Your personal energy is being constantly created and nurtured by source energy. Source energy moves through you *and is you. You feel your emotions becoming quiet and peaceful. The dense energy that brings form to your body becomes lighter, thinner, and the boundaries loosen. The loose energy continues to expand, and the space within and between the cells, molecules, and atoms becomes voluminous. In that space, high frequency bundles of energy dissolve the last traces of form, and you become infinite space filled with energy. You are an energy being without form. Your thoughts drift away, and your mind becomes a distant observer of the unity and power of complete oneness. You are nothing and you are everything. You are energy. Experience yourself as radiant source energy for as long as you have time by maintaining the focus of your attention on the energy.*

When you are ready to return, gradually notice your physical form, thoughts, and emotions returning to your awareness. Try to stay as blended with source energy as you can. Gratefully thank the void and the source energy for this opportunity to blend. Breathing deeply of the powerful source energy of the void to bring it back with you, you reach to your side, pull the cord that opens the parachute, and begin to descend back into your soft space and your body. With every number counted from ten to one, you become more awake and more alert, being fully awake and alert at the number one. Ten, gently begin your journey back to Earth by descending through the void, back into the cosmos; nine, eight, seven, six, drifting back into our universe; five, four, back into the Earth's atmosphere; three, back into the sky and becoming more awake; two, one, back into your body, fully awake and alert, and feeling better than you have in a long, long time. Try to stay open for as long as you can, and remain aware of the different sensations you are having.

Sit quietly for a few moments and reflect on your experience. Be gentle with yourself as you wiggle and stretch, becoming fully present in your body and conscious mind. Express your experience, thoughts, and feelings in your journal.

MEDITATION

Return to Source

Sit in quiet contemplation in your nature place or in a soft space where you will not be disturbed. Open your mind and relax. Allow any distracting thoughts to drift away. Notice them and let them go.

Observe, notice, experience, sense, and feel everything about yourself. Focus your attention on your emotions. Notice what you are feeling. Focus your attention on your thoughts. Notice what you are thinking. Focus your attention on your body. Notice what you are experiencing physically. Focus your attention on your energy field. Notice what you are feeling energetically. Focus your attention on your soul. Notice what you are feeling spiritually. Send your awareness down inside of yourself and notice your source energy. Experience the energy that created you and sustains your life. Continue to sit quietly and observe your source energy for a while.

When you are ready, shift your attention to observe the place where you are sitting. Notice, see, sense, feel, and experience everything about this place. Notice what you see. Notice the physical objects of the place. Are there any elements that you notice? If it's outdoors, is the wind blowing or the sun shining? If it's indoors, is there a candle burning or a water fountain trickling in the corner? Notice if there is any movement. Notice what you smell. Notice what emotions this place elicits. Relax and soften your eyes, and continue to observe for a while. Allow yourself to sense and feel the source energy of this place. Allow yourself to sense and feel the source energy of each individual object. Allow yourself to experience the source energy of all the objects collectively in this place. Allow yourself to sense and feel the energy that created and sustains this place. Breathe deeply of this energy. Notice your sensations.

Now close your eyes and allow your inner wisdom to bubble forth. Relax, focus, and feel. Open up to feeling all the source energy around and in this place, including your own. Allow questions and answers to form in and out of your thoughts. Questions like: What is source energy?

Where does source energy come from? Is my personal energy affected by the source energy of this place and the objects here? Are we made up of the same source energy? If so, then why do we look, feel, and behave differently? Does the combination of the elements and the other energies here affect the source energy of this place? Is this place alive? Does the source energy affect all of the things that are here? Do the objects in this place have a soul? Do they have a spirit? Are the soul and spirit source energy? Or something different? How can you tell? Are your soul and spirit made of source energy? What makes your soul and spirit different from someone else's?

Stay in this place in contemplation for as long as you have time, asking your own questions of yourself. When you are ready, take in a deep breath and allow yourself a few moments to shift your awareness back to ordinary life and fully integrate back into your body.

EXERCISES TO RETURN TO SOURCE

If you're experiencing low energy or feeling disconnected from yourself, others, your world, or the powers that be, these returning to source exercises will have you resonating with the energizing potential of the life-force within minutes. They can be performed anywhere, at any time, since you do not need to enter into an altered state of consciousness for them to be effective. Practice these exercises whenever you are in need, or, if you have the time and are in an appropriate place, for added relaxation and receptivity you may choose to enter into an altered state of consciousness, as described in chapter one, before practicing these exercises.

Center of the Earth Void and the Center of the Internal Void

The Center of the Earth Void and the Center of the Internal Void exercises are similar to previous guided journeys that took you to the source energy in the "outer space external void." Just as there is a void "out there" above us, there is also a void "down there" below us. And just as there are external voids out there, there is an internal void within us.

Mystics have long understood the relationship between all things, and shared this knowing with us through the saying, "As above, so below; as without, so within." These exercises can also be performed as a journey by using the Universal Induction.

Begin by taking in a deep breath, relaxing, and closing your eyes. Let go of your everyday thoughts and concerns. Feel your mind quiet and your whole self become calm and peaceful. When you feel relaxed, if you are doing the Center of the Earth Void exercise, send your awareness down into the center of the earth. Deep within the solid rock and mass of the Earth is a void—an open space teeming with creative, potential source energy. Go to that place. If you are doing the Center of the Internal Void exercise, send your awareness down into the center of yourself. Deep within your soul, beyond the numerous systems of flesh, bones, organs, nerves, and cells, is a void—an open space teeming with creative, potential source energy. Go to that place. Relax, be patient with yourself, and when you find yourself in the void, use all of your senses to experience it, and then blend with the source energy there.

Feel yourself suspended in the infinite and boundless void. You notice that there are no forms here, but a sensation of fullness permeates your awareness. Opening your senses further, you begin to resonate with the pure high vibrational force that is source energy. You can feel it around you and throughout the vastness of the void. You feel it moving through you, entering on your breath and swirling through your body and energy field.

People's experiences in the various voids differ, so take a few moments to notice what it is like for you. Notice if it is dark or light, if it is deep darkness, soft darkness, bright light, gentle light, velvety darkness teeming with tiny twinkling lights, or a soft light filled with minute dark spots. Be aware of everything that you see, smell, taste, feel, sense, and experience. Feel the creative potential of the source energy, and simultaneously sense the nothingness and the everythingness. Think about the words that we use to describe source energy, like the divine, the one, the source, the truth, the light, pure love, Godliness, and so on. Notice how each of these names resonates for you, and how each of these names resonates with the energy in the void. There is no right or wrong, so relax and experience whatever it is that you are experiencing.

When you are ready, begin to dissolve the dense energy that creates the physical form of your body. Experience yourself becoming lighter and thinner as your boundaries loosen. The loose energy continues to expand, and the space within and between your cells, molecules, and atoms becomes voluminous. In that space, high frequency bundles of energy dissolve the last traces of form, and you become infinite space filled with energy. You are an energy being without form. Your thoughts drift away, and your mind becomes a distant observer of the unity and power of complete oneness. You are nothing, and you are everything. You are energy. Experience yourself as radiant source energy for as long as you have time by maintaining the focus of your attention on the energy.

Stay in this place in contemplation for as long as you have time. When you are ready, take in a deep breath and allow yourself a few moments to shift your awareness back to ordinary life and fully integrate back into your body. When you have time, record your experience in your journal.

Nature

Because nature is the perfect expression of source energy, this next exercise utilizes the direct link that innately exists between nature and source energy to help you return to source.

Go to a place in nature, sit down, and make yourself comfortable. Take in a deep breath and allow your mind to become quiet. Allow any distracting thoughts to drift away. Notice them and let them go. Shift your attention away from your everyday life concerns, and be present in the moment. Observe, notice, experience, sense, and feel everything about yourself right here, right now. And then let it all go. Shift your focus away from yourself. Be in this place of nature as fully as possible. Observe, notice, experience, sense, and feel everything about this place where you are sitting.

When you are ready, choose an object to blend with, such a tree, a lake, or a rock. Ask permission to blend with it, and if you sense it giving you permission, blend by either sending your energy into its energy field or inviting its energy into your energy field. Once you have merged, fully experience yourself in its energy. Feel what it feels like to be this being. When you are ready, dissolve yourself into its source energy. Feel your form and your boundaries fall away as you become nature.

Remain blended for as long as you have time. When you are ready, take in a deep breath and allow yourself a few moments to shift your awareness back to ordinary life and fully integrate back into your body. Record your experience in your journal when you have time.

Heart Meditation

The Heart Meditation exercise helps you to fully immerse yourself in, and then become, the pure love that is source energy.

Begin by taking in a deep breath, relaxing, and closing your eyes. Let go of your everyday thoughts and concerns. Feel your mind quiet and your whole self become calm and peaceful. Allow any distracting thoughts to drift away. Notice them and let them go. Shift your attention away from your everyday life concerns, and be present in the moment.

When you feel relaxed and ready, focus your attention on your heart. Take in a deep breath, and feel the source energy of the universe and the divine tell you, "I love you!" Receive that message fully with your heart, and feel the pure love of creation warming and nurturing your whole being. On your next exhalation, send a heartfelt "I love you!" from your whole being, heart, and soul to the source energy of the universe and the divine. Continue this pattern of receiving and sending love on each inhalation and exhalation for as many cycles as you would like. Notice *that you and the universal source are creating a circle of pure love that gradually erases separateness.*

When you need to return to your ordinary activities, don't disengage. Allow the cycle to continue at the edge of your conscious awareness.

Spirit Guide Assistance

In the Spirit Guide Assistance exercise, you will have the opportunity to ask a Spirit Guide to help you return to source. This may occur in varied ways depending upon the energy or personal preference of you or your Spirit Guide. You may blend with it, as you did with an object in the Nature exercise, or you may travel to a place above, below, or within to blend with "internal" or "external" source energy. Where you go or how you do it doesn't matter—any way or place that makes it easy for you to connect and then become source energy is correct.

Begin by taking in a deep breath, relaxing, and closing your eyes. Let go of your everyday thoughts and concerns. Feel your mind quiet and your whole self become calm and peaceful. Allow any distracting thoughts to drift away. Notice them and let them go. Shift your attention away from your everyday life concerns, and be present in the moment.

Become aware of the presence of a Spirit Guide. Ask it to help you blend with source energy in whatever way and in whatever place works best for it and for you. Let go of any expectations, and allow yourself to go, be, and do. Experience this mini journey with all of your senses. Relax, imagine, explore. When you are ready, become source energy by dissolving yourself.

Remain source energy for as long as you have time. When you are ready, take in a deep breath, and allow yourself a few moments to shift your awareness back to ordinary life and fully integrate back into your body. Record your experience in your journal when time permits.

Advanced Rainbow Fountain

As you learned in chapter 5, the Rainbow Fountain of Energy exercise entails drawing in universal life-force energy from the Earth and the infinite universe. We now know that these powerful energies are rooted in source energy. The Advanced Rainbow Fountain exercise draws in source energy from the Earth and universe, and mixes it with your source energy to create a rainbow fountain. Once the rainbow fountain is flowing and expanded out into your energy field, the energy of it is used to help you dissolve yourself into it to become source energy. Also, instead of bringing your rainbow fountain back into your body at the end of the exercise, the Advanced Rainbow Fountain exercise has you return to your ordinary activities, remaining potent source energy. This exercise provides a powerful means to become whole, one with all of life, empowered, and energized. The Advanced Rainbow Fountain exercise is included on the accompanying CD as it is written here.

Stand with your feet hip-distance apart, arms down at your sides. Close your eyes, and take in a deep breath. Keep breathing deeply throughout the exercise, using your breath, physical movement, and intention to draw in and move the energy. Allow yourself to relax. Slip into an altered state of consciousness if you choose. Place your attention on the soles of your feet and the crown of your head. Take in a deep breath, reach for the floor, and draw in the strong, grounding energy of the Earth. Feel it slowly moving up your feet and legs into your root chakra as you roll back up and place your hands on your root chakra. Raise your arms above your head. Take in a deep breath, and draw in the universal life-force energy from above you as you bring your hands down over your head and face. Feel the energy melting in through the top of your head and flowing down into your root chakra as you bring your hands down over your body and place them on your root chakra. Where these two energies meet, see the chakra ignite with a deep, vibrant red energy. See, sense, and feel that red ball of energy grow and expand, becoming a radiant source of glowing, ruby-red light that begins to saturate all of the tissues in your body. See, sense, and feel this light soaking into your abdomen, chest, head, and out of your arms, bathing organs, muscle, blood, and bone until your entire body becomes a great neon beacon of this light. After a few moments, allow that ruby-red energy to recede once again back to its home in your root chakra, where it continues to glow and spin brightly.

Take in a deep breath, reach for the floor, and draw in the strong, grounding energy of the Earth. Feel it slowly moving up your feet and legs and into your sacral chakra as you roll back up and place your hands on your sacral chakra. Raise your arms above your head. Take in a deep breath and draw in the universal life-force energy from above as you bring your hands down over your head and face. Feel the energy melting in through the top of your head and flowing down into your sacral chakra as you bring your hands down over your body and place them on your sacral chakra. These two energies combine, spin, and glow here with a bright orange light. See, sense, and feel that orange ball of light grow and expand, becoming a radiant source of glowing, bright orange light that begins to saturate all of the tissues in your body. See, sense, and feel this light soaking into your abdomen, chest, head, and out your arms, bathing organs, muscle, blood, and bone until your entire body becomes a great neon beacon of this light. Stir this energy and expand it throughout your body, saturating every cell with this orange, regenerative light. After a few moments, shrink the light back into its home in your sacral chakra, where it continues to spin and glow a brilliant orange.

Take in a deep breath, reach fo the floor, and draw in the strong, grounding energy of the Earth. Feel it slowly moving up your feet and legs and into your solar plexus as you roll back up and place your hands on your solar plexus. Raise your arms above your head. Take in a deep breath, and draw in the universal life-force energy from above as you bring your hands down over your head and face. Feel the energy melting in through the top of your head and flowing down into your solar plexus as you bring your hands down over your body and place them on your solar plexus. These two energies combine, spin, and glow here with a bright, sunshine-yellow light. See, sense, and feel that yellow ball of energy grow and expand, becoming a radiant source of glowing, bright yellow light that begins to saturate all of the tissues in your body. See, sense, and feel this light soaking into your abdomen, chest, head, and out your arms, bathing organs, muscle, blood, and bone until your entire body becomes a great neon beacon of this light. Stir this energy and expand it throughout your body, saturating every cell with this sunshine-yellow, regenerative light. After a few moments, shrink the light to its home in your solar plexus, where it continues to spin and glow a bright sunshine-yellow.

Take in a deep breath, reach for the floor, and draw in the strong, grounding energy of the Earth. Feel it slowly moving up your feet and legs and into your heart chakra as you roll back up and place your hands on your heart chakra. Raise your arms above your head. Take in a deep breath, and draw in the universal life-force energy from above as you bring your hands down over your head and face. Feel the energy melting in through the top of your head and flowing down into your heart chakra as you bring your hands down over your body and place them on your heart chakra. These two energies combine, spin, and glow here with an emerald-green light. See, sense, and feel that emerald-green ball of energy grow and expand, becoming a radiant source of glowing, emerald-green light that begins to saturate all of the tissues in your body. See, sense, and feel this light soaking into your abdomen, chest, head, and out your arms, bathing organs, muscle, blood, and bone until your entire body becomes a great neon beacon of this light. Stir this energy and expand it throughout your body, saturating every cell with this emerald-green, regenerative light. After a few moments, shrink the light back to its home in your heart chakra, where it continues to spin and glow an emerald-green.

Take in a deep breath, reach for the floor, and draw in the strong, grounding energy of the Earth. Feel it slowly moving up your feet and legs and into your throat chakra as you roll back up and place your hands on your throat chakra. Raise your arms above your head. Take in a deep breath, and draw in the universal life-force energy from above as you bring your hands down over your head and face. Feel the energy melting in through the top of your head and flowing down into your throat chakra as you bring your hands down over your head and place them on your throat chakra. These two energies combine, spin, and glow here with a deep azure-blue. See, sense, and feel that azure-blue ball of energy grow and expand, becoming a radiant source of glowing, deep azure-blue light that begins to saturate all of the tissues in your body. See, sense, and feel this light soaking into your abdomen, chest, head, and out your arms, bathing organs, muscle, blood, and bone until your entire body becomes a great neon beacon of this light. Stir this energy and expand it through your body, saturating every cell with this azure-blue, regenerative light. After a few moments, shrink this light back to its home in your throat chakra, where it continues to spin and glow a deep azure-blue.

Take in a deep breath, reach for the floor, and draw in the strong, grounding energy of the Earth. Feel it slowly moving up your feet and legs and into your third-eye chakra as you roll back up and place your hands on your third-eye chakra. Raise your arms above your head. Take in a deep breath, and draw in the universal life-force energy from above as you bring your hands down over your head. Feel the energy melting in through the top of your head and flowing down into your third-eye chakra as you bring your hands down over your third-eye chakra. These two energies combine, spin, and glow here with an indigo-purple light. See, sense, and feel that indigo ball of energy grow and expand, becoming a radiant source of glowing, deep indigo light that begins to saturate all of the tissues in your body. See, sense, and feel this light soaking into your abdomen, chest, head, and out your arms, bathing organs, muscle, blood, and bone until your entire body becomes a great neon beacon of this light. Stir this energy and expand it throughout your body, saturating every cell with this indigo, regenerative light. After a few moments, shrink the light back to its home in your third-eye chakra, where it continues to spin and glow a deep indigo-purple.

Take in a deep breath, reach for the floor, and draw in the strong, grounding energy of the Earth. Feel it slowly moving up your feet and legs into your crown chakra as you roll back up and place your hands on your crown chakra. Raise your arms above your head. Take in a deep breath, and draw in the universal life-force energy from above as you bring your hands down to the top of your head. Feel the energy melting down into your crown chakra. These two energies combine, spin, and glow here with a pale violet light. See, sense, and feel this violet ball of energy grow and expand, becoming a radiant source of glowing, pale violet light that begins to saturate all of the tissues in your body. See, sense, and feel this light soaking into your abdomen, chest, head, and out your arms, bathing organs, muscle, blood, and bone until your entire body becomes a great neon beacon of this light. Stir this energy and expand it throughout your body, saturating every cell with this violet, regenerative light. After a few moments, shrink the light back to its home in your crown chakra, where it continues to spin and glow a pale violet.

When all seven chakras have been energized, continue to see and feel them spinning and glowing in each of their homes, washing and energizing all of your tissues. See, sense, and feel the swirling bright light of the universal life-force surrounding your body. See, sense, and feel the swirling maroon of the Earth energy beneath you. On your next inhalation, draw the bright light and maroon of the universal and Earth energies into your body and chakras. As the universal and Earth energies blend with your chakra energies, a radiant, internal rainbow glows in the center of your body, extending from your feet to your head.

Using your breath, body movement, and intention, reach down, and as you inhale deeply, draw the rainbow energy up through your feet, legs, and body. As you roll up to standing, place your hands on your solar plexus and exhale. On your next inhalation, sweep your hands and arms up over your body and over your head, drawing the rainbow energy through your body and head. As you exhale, let the rainbow energy flow out the top of your head, like a water fountain, and spill down around you as you sweep your arms out and down to your sides. See, sense, and *feel the power of the colorful energies rushing up through your body like an internal geyser. As the energy exits your head, see, sense, and feel a rainbow cascade out to the limits of your energy field and down again to your feet. As the rainbow mists through your energy field, see, sense, and feel your body cleansed and refreshed by the movement of this energy. Using your inhalations, body movements, and intention, continue drawing up the rainbow energy at your own pace. Feel it spill out into your energy field and back to the Earth on your exhalations. Repeat at least six times, and continue the energy movement until your body, and the luminous egg that is your energy field, are completely energized.*

When you are ready, expand the vibrant, swirling rainbow energy all the way out beyond your energy boundary, allowing your boundaries, energy field, and body to blend into the dynamic, sparkling source energy of the universe. Allow your emotions to become calm and tranquil. Using your intention, allow the dense energy form that makes up your body to become porous and open. Experience the space within and between your cells, molecules, and atoms expanding. High vibrational energy bundles race around, opening up infinite space. You are energy. You are an energy being without form. You are vibrant, swirling color. Your thoughts slip away, and your mind becomes a distant witness to the unity and power of complete oneness.

When you are finished and ready to return to your ordinary activities, take in a deep breath and open your eyes. Notice how you feel cleansed and energy-filled. There is no need to shut down the circulating energies around and through you. Try to stay open for as long as you can, and remain aware of the different sensations you are having. Energy in motion stays in motion, so the benefits of this exercise continue long after you have finished it.

• • •

The invisible energies that create, sustain, and invigorate life are real and readily accessible. By opening your mind, senses, and energy field to these energies regularly, you will sparkle with the potent vitality inherent within them. The only way to feel energized is to keep your energy dynamic. The way to keep your energy dynamic is to activate your personal energy and refresh it often with universal life-force, and spiritual and source energy. All of the energy that you want and need is available to you through the activities that you have learned throughout this book. You have the tools; now, to have energy for life, you just need to make it happen. Chapter 8 is full of ideas and tips that will help you easily integrate energy into your everyday life.

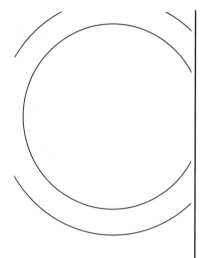

EIGHT

Energy for Life

*The quieter
You become,
The more
You can hear.*
~Baba Ram Dass

The best way to be energized is to stay energized. The best way to stay energized is to stimulate your personal energy and refresh it often with universal life-force, and spiritual and source energy. Energy is the sustenance that feeds your body, mind, emotions, and soul, and is the key to reclaiming and maintaining your life-force. An infinite amount of vibrant energy is already inside of you and available just outside of you if you make the effort and the choice to utilize it. The level of vibrancy and quality of your vitality depend on how strong your commitment is to yourself about being energized and healthy. The activities that I have selected to share within the pages of this book and the meditations on the accompanying CD are the best that I have discovered for reviving and maintaining high levels of energy. By practicing these on a regular basis you will be radiant and vibrant.

CREATING AN ENERGIZING PRACTICE

Energizing yourself begins with a simple but powerful commitment. When the right circumstances within you create, draw in, and maintain energy, you feel energetic. You already have the tools and the abilities to set up these circumstances, but your commitment is the key, because without it, nothing changes. You can read books, you can dabble in energizing activities, you can attend workshops, you can receive energy healings from therapists, but until you decide that you are important and your energy is your priority, the effects of your dabblings will remain impotent and vitality will evade you. The activities detailed in this book are powerful life-changing energizers, and they are here for your use. You are worth it, so go ahead, sit back, take in a deep breath, and relax while you make this important pledge to yourself.

Take a few moments to quiet your mind and relax your body. Allow your muscles to become loose and relaxed, limp and heavy. Relax your shoulders, your neck, and your face. Feel the tension and stress float away like soft puffs of smoke. Allow any thoughts to drift away on cottony summer clouds and your mind to empty into the clear blue sky. In this quiet, clear

state of mind, commit to yourself that you will practice at least one ener-
gizing activity per day to the best of your ability. Pledge that right now,
from this point forward, you are making your health and vitality a prior-
ity, and that you commit to making yourself whole. Take in another deep
breath, and relax. Congratulations, you have taken the most important
step. You have decided to make yourself important and to commit to
energy for life!

Now that you have made the commitment, the next step is to do it. You, and only you, are the recipient of all of the effort that you put into your energizing practice. It's like receiving a 300 percent return on an investment. This profit margin is unheard of in the business world, but true in the world of energy. You reap what you sow! Whatever you put in, you receive back at least threefold because your mind, emotions, body, energy field, and soul want to be healthy and in balance. So do yourself a favor and put in all that you can. You'll be amazed at how vital you will feel.

Set aside at least fifteen to twenty minutes in one sitting per day, every day, to practice the energizing activity of your choice. The benefits of committing to, and maintaining, a regular practice are multifold, and the importance cannot be overstated. A regular preset time helps you to keep your commitment to yourself by providing routine and consistency. Make an appointment with yourself to practice. This goes a long way in helping you to make it happen!

It might seem easy to commit to just a few minutes a day, but you may find it a little more difficult to actually carve this out of your busy life. This is when the stability of a regular practice helps your will to override distractions or complacency. You will also find that after a few days of regular practice the mere act of going into the space where you practice triggers the relaxation and energizing process. Your psyche becomes conditioned and knows what to expect when you enter into your practice room, and will automatically begin to respond. You will find that this makes it easier for you to go deeper with each practice session. The cumulative effect of your practice keeps the energy flowing, and each practice session builds on the last ones.

Don't hesitate to practice the same activities over and over and over again. The more you practice, the more powerful the results will be. Don't think that because you have practiced an activity once or twice and it was either awesome or it didn't work that you are finished exploring the possibilities of that activity. Some people in my workshops find that they have not been able to open up to much energy with certain activities until they have practiced them several or many times. All of a sudden a breakthrough energy shift occurs that brings that person a flood of powerful energy, and that particular activity becomes a regularly used favorite. If you have favorites already, great, but don't forget to keep trying others.

Your energy practice is a quiet, contemplative time that needs to be focused and disciplined. When practicing any of the activities it is critically important to do more than just visualize. You need to use all of your senses to effectively experience the energy. As you visualize whatever exercise you are doing, sit quietly with the visualizations and feel the energy run through you and around you; hear it, taste it, smell it, and see it.

It is important that you create a daily energy practice that works for you. You need to make it personal to you and valuable for you. It should be pleasurable and something that you enjoy. If you look forward to your daily ritual, you are more likely to follow through with your commitment to participate each day. You may choose to vary your methods from day to day depending on how you feel and what appeals to you that day, or you may benefit from a routine that is the same each day. Call in your Spirit Guides to empower your practice if you would like. Whichever activity you choose, keep your practice sharp and dynamic. Be creative and honor your feelings and desires each day. Your special energizing time needs to be nurturing, fun, exciting, adventurous, and healing.

Keep it simple. I can't emphasize this enough. When things become complicated and cumbersome we usually end up setting them aside, believing that they didn't work for us. These energizing activities will work for you, but you must do them, and the more regularly you practice them the more benefits you will experience. If you keep it simple and enjoyable, you will come to cherish your few minutes a day of nourishing you time. As you create energy and peace in your body and your life through your daily practice, you will begin to notice that it becomes easier and easier to stay energized, strong, and healthy.

Working the Program

Follow your energizing practice as consistently as you can every day for at least thirty days. A consistent energizing practice, integrated with mindful awareness and energy connecting activities throughout the day, every day, changes lives. I have seen it time and time again. Those who work the program are able to energize. Those who let it slide are unable to become, or maintain the power to stay, energized. If you nurture yourself by practicing the energizing activities daily for at least thirty days, you *will* experience change.

Do whatever it takes to follow through with your commitments to yourself. Share your practices and experiences with friends and family, and open your mind to new ideas. Experiment, have fun, and be willing to try things that seem a little hokey to you at first. You won't know what might work best for you until you have given it a fair shake. Because you are unique, some methods may be more beneficial for you than others, but be sure to allow yourself ample time and space to fully explore what works best for you.

Avoid becoming complacent, and do whatever you can to prevent and override distractions. No matter how firm your commitment and dedication, your practice will be challenged from time to time. Life doesn't stop just because it's your set-aside time to go into your soft space to practice an energizing activity. Of course, it helps to designate a time when there will be the least possible amount of distractions, but even then, life happens, so when this occurs, relax, take in a deep breath, and allow yourself to choose the best course of action. Remember your commitment to yourself to make your energizing practice one of your priorities. Frequently, the things, people, or your own feelings and resistances that attempt to distract you can wait a few minutes, and you need to be firm in your conviction to take care of yourself. However, if something demands immediate attention and you are unable to practice at your designated time that day, try to do it later in the day; break the session up into smaller increments, and infuse them throughout the day, or simply resume your practice the next day.

Do not become guilt-ridden and obsessive about your practice. There is a big difference between commitment and rigidity. The purpose of your practice is to become relaxed, calm, still, aware, and connected with energy. Obsessing will only pull you further away from your intentions, so relax and flow with life, nurturing and energizing yourself along the way. If your practice slacks off a bit, pick up wherever you left off and start again. Begin again, and again, and again if that is what you need to do.

Energize Throughout the Day

Durrette, a friend and client, shares: "Doing massage and energy work on clients several times a week motivates me to keep in tune with my own body. It's easy for body workers to either give away their vital energy or take on the cast-off energy of others. I use the shielding to prevent this.

"I also prepare myself energetically by doing the Rainbow Waterfall exercise while showering. This easily clears out unwanted energy that I may pick up or create with my own life experiences. I use a variety of ways to power up with energy several times a day. When I'm tired between clients, I might do something simple like deep breathing or spinning in a circle. If I have time, I'll journey or do the Rainbow Fountain exercise. I'm fortunate to be an old student of Colleen's, and have learned many of these activities over the years. These exercises enrich my life by giving me strength in my body, mind, and soul to do the work I love. After working, I ground myself and my clients. Grounding helps me to be centered and present, here on Mother Earth. Grounding helps me to observe life around me and be present to interact with it. After several massages, I often feel pleasantly disconnected. Once, after six hours of work, I skipped out of my treatment room, forgetting to ground. I took a tumble that my body felt for months. Grounding is something I no longer forget. Recently, I learned the Inversion Energy Awareness exercise. This also helps me to release the energy that is not mine and revitalizes my energy. It allows me to express love and gratitude for the day, and helps me to be my individual self within the Universal Oneness."

Many of these activities have been successfully shared with my clients.

Staying energized is a continual process and a way of life, not just a one-time-a-day practice. You use up and give out enormous amounts of energy all day long, so it is imperative that you replenish yourself with the extraordinary energy that is available to you throughout the day.

Be sure to give yourself several three-to-five minute energizing breaks throughout your day to quiet your mind, relax your muscles, and replenish your energy. Any of the energy connecting exercises will keep your energy levels high, release blockages, and seal leakages before these problems become debilitating. If you have time and are in an appropriate place, do one of the guided journeys to help you relax even more while you energize or listen to the CD.

No matter how busy you may be or how rigid your schedule, you can easily energize using any of the energy connecting exercises taught in this book. I suggest integrating a variety of them into your everyday life in small, powerful increments. You can use these exercises to begin your day, as a work break, any time you feel stressed, when you feel fatigued to restore your energy, just before leaving work to rejuvenate, or in the evening to relax. To keep your energy flowing vibrantly, remember to use them whenever you have a few spare moments.

In our busy world of time crunching and stress, we sometimes make our lives even more stressful by trying to add good things into our already overwhelmingly busy lives. Sometimes what we need to do is add the good things into the other things that we are already doing. Exercise time is one of those times. It is my favorite time to fill with energy. Any repetitive workout such as running, yoga, or using indoor machines like a treadmill, elliptical, or stationary bike can have extra value added by incorporating an energy connecting exercise. My friend Chris, who teaches bicycle spinning classes in Cincinnati, informed me that the spinning workout was developed by a man with attention deficit hyperactive disorder as a means for meditation. Because he found it impossible to meditate while sitting still, he created spinning to provide a safe, indoor, nontraveling mode of repetitive movement to help him relax and empty his thoughts.

You can do the same with any activity that does not require you to be alert and watchful for things like traffic or a ball coming at you. Any repetitive movement or routine daily activity where you are safe from harm is a great time for you to energize. Instead of engaging in self-defeating thoughts or circular mind games, make this time productive with mindful energizing intention. By focusing your mind on an energy connecting exercise while doing routine activities like folding clothes, mowing the lawn, or exercising, you can ensure that your energy reserves are being replenished throughout the day.

Likewise, downtime can be transformed into energize time. Downtime is typically one of those annoying little life incidents that drains our energy. Naturally occurring downtime moments like sitting at a traffic light or waiting for your next appointment can be changed from a frustrating waste of time and energy to an energy connecting break. The key is to shift your mind away from your normal mental chatter and into an energy connecting exercise.

Maintaining an energy connection helps you to remain aware of what is happening in your energy field, body, mind, emotions, and soul. With greater awareness, you will more easily sense when you feel out of sync or when something out of the ordinary is pulling on your energy. By becoming aware of this imbalance more quickly, you can then identify the sources, situations, places, people, and internal triggers and reactions that deplete your energy sooner. In so doing, you can take appropriate steps to vanquish this drain from your life or protect yourself by activating your personal energy or drawing in more universal and spiritual energy to fortify yourself, preventing destructive depletion.

To avoid energy loss, your best line of defense is power-filling every day. "An ounce of prevention beats a pound of cure," as they say. By boosting your energy every day, you build an impenetrable boundary of personal power over time. Constant awareness of yourself and your energy adds to that code of preventive cure. If you feel that your energy is being drained or attacked, take the time to activate your energy field and fill with powerful universal and Spirit energy as soon as possible. If you have the time, take ten to twenty minutes to sit down, quiet yourself, and journey or meditate.

If not, I recommend using one of the protection shield exercises in addition to the Strong Mountain and Rainbow Fountain exercises described in chapter five. Both of these exercises are effective methods for boosting your personal power that set up a natural internal shield of resilient energy. If you feel dirtied or congested by an attack or the stresses of everyday life, the Rainbow Waterfall exercise is an excellent way to cleanse your energy field.

If you find that you are having difficulty staying aware of your energy, it is important that you train yourself to check in periodically to assess your energy connection and flow. It is easy to remember to do this by creating habits in your routine that become conditioned reminders. Setting up objects that trigger your awareness, like positioning a statue in a certain room or hanging a crystal in your car, will help remind you to check in with yourself every time the objects catch your eye. Posting notes around your frequented environments is also helpful. Regular use of these reminders also helps you become accustomed to connecting with energy, and as you feel the benefits, the process maintains its own momentum without much thought.

Paying attention to your energy levels throughout the day takes no extra time. And it doesn't need to take any extra time out of your busy day to feel the presence of universal life-force and Spirit energy, to observe the beauty of nature and the world around you, and to run energy through your body. What it does require is internal quietness, bare awareness, mind focus, and the discipline to make it happen. You need only stop the chatter of your mind to be able to listen and feel, to focus and become aware. It is not difficult to do these things, but you must remember to do them.

"What you give energy to, you give life to."

By paying attention to yourself you give yourself energy, and by doing this, you give yourself life. The following story eloquently illustrates this point . . .

> *A Native American grandfather was talking to his grandson about how he felt. He said, "I feel as if I have two wolves fighting in my heart. One wolf is the vengeful, angry, violent one. The other is the loving, compassionate one." The grandson asked him, "Which wolf will win the fight in your heart?" The grandfather answered, "The one I feed."*

Which wolf will you choose to feed, the wolf of imbalance and low energy or the wolf of balance and vibrant energy? If you feed your fatigue by maintaining the imbalances or behaviors that exacerbate your condition, the wolf of fatigue will win over the wolf of energy. This will happen even if it is not a conscious act on your part. Ultimately, the choice is yours. And the results rest in the fortitude of your own conviction. Go ahead. Give it to yourself. You are worth it! Energize yourself every day!

• • •

Sit back, take in a deep breath, close your eyes, and relax. Activate the power of your imagination and your awareness. Imagine yourself completely energized. Imagine what this is like. Imagine what it looks like. Imagine what it feels like. Become aware that this is already happening within you.

By energizing yourself with the activities presented in this book and CD, important shifts have been taking place in your energy levels and your world. The changes are subtle and woven throughout the tapestry of everyday life. It seems like nothing has changed, yet it feels like everything has changed. Externally, life looks similar to what it has always been, yet it is profoundly different, because inside, you are different. This change is energy.

You notice feeling less fatigue and energy loss. You notice that you are feeling good all day. The way you make choices is different because of your abundant energy. You feel like participating more actively in the things you enjoy and making healthy choices for yourself. Life seems to flow more smoothly, and your energy levels are less affected by the ups and downs of the outside world. It is easy to follow through with your energizing practice, and you miss it if you have to skip a day. The little steps are going a long way toward making big differences in your life. Now, imagine that all of this is really true.

Be aware that it is all really true, and it is happening inside of you right now. Give yourself a pat on the back for having the desire and inner fortitude to achieve energy for life. You are energized—feel it!

APPENDIX

RECOMMENDED READING, MOVIES, AND MUSIC

There are many good books on the subjects and activities I have described in *Energy for Life*. The books listed here are those that I have personally read and recommend. The titles with the stars next to them are books that I recommend for general ease of content and understanding for the beginner. Know that this list is not all-inclusive of the many informative books available.

Energy/Quantum Physics

* *The Little Book of Bleeps: Quotations from the Movie What the Bleep Do We Know!?*. First edition. Yelm, Wash.: Captured Light Distribution, 2004.

Greene, R. Brian. *The Elegant Universe*. First Vintage Books edition. New York: Vintage Books, 2003.

* Wilber, Ken. *Kosmic Consciousness*. Audio tapes. Unabridged edition. Boulder, Colo.: Sounds True, 2003.

Wolf, Fred Alan. *Dr. Quantum Presents: A User's Guide to Your Universe*. Audio tapes. Boulder, Colo.: Sounds True, 2005.

Energy Healing

* Brennan, Barbara. *Hands of Light*. New York: Bantam Books, 1987.

Eden, Donna. *Energy Medicine*. New York: Putnam Publishing Group, 2000.

* Ritberger, Carol. *Your Personality, Your Health: Connecting Personality with the Human Energy System, Chakras, and Wellness*. Carlsbad, Calif.: The Hay House, Inc., 1998.

Mind / Body Healing

BoDine, Echo L. *Passion to Heal.* Mill Valley, Calif.: Nataraj Publishing, 1993.

* Deatsman, Colleen. *Inner Power.* St. Paul, Minn.: Llewellyn Publications, 2005.

* Hay, Louise L. *The Power Is Within You.* Carson, Calif.: The Hay House, Inc., 1991.

* ———. *You Can Heal Your Life.* Carson, Calif.: The Hay House, Inc., 1987.

* Hendricks, Gay. *Conscious Breathing.* New York: Bantam Books, 1995.

Sanders, Laurie G., and Melvin J. Tucker. *Centering.* Second edition. Rochester, Vt.: Destiny Books, 1993.

* Topt, Linda Noble. *You Are Not Your Illness.* New York: Fireside / Simon & Schuster, 1995.

Enlightenment / Mastering Life

Braden, Gregg. *Speaking the Lost Language of God: Awakening the Forgotten Wisdom of Prayer, Prophecy, and the Dead Sea Scrolls.* Niles, Ill.: Nightingale Conant, 2004.

* Campbell, Joseph. *Man and Myth.* Audio tapes. St. Paul, Minn.: High Bridge Co., 1998.

* Chodron, Pema. *When Things Fall Apart.* Boston: Shambhala, 1997.

Chopra, Deepak. *The Return of Merlin.* New York: Harmony Books, 1995.

* ———. *The Way of the Wizard.* New York: Harmony Books, 1995.

Easwaran, Eknath. *Your Life Is Your Message.* New York: Hyperion, 1992.

* Elliot, William. *Tying Rocks to Clouds: Meetings and Conversations with Wise and Spiritual People.* Wheaton, Ill.: Quest Books, 1995.

Epstein, Mark. *Going to Pieces Without Falling Apart.* New York: Broadway Books, 1998.

* Free, Pamela J. *Come Home to Your Body.* St. Paul, Minn.: Llewellyn Publications, 1997.

Jacobson, Leonard. *Embracing the Present.* A Conscious Living Publication, 1997.

———. *Words from Silence.* A Conscious Living Publication, 1991.

Kabat-Zinn, Jon. *Coming to Our Senses.* New York: Hyperion, 2005.

* ———. *Wherever You Go There You Are.* New York: Hyperion, 1994.

* Millman, Dan. *Everyday Enlightenment.* New York: Warner Books, Inc., 1999.

* ———. *Way of the Peaceful Warrior: A Book that Changes Lives.* 20th Edition. Novato, Calif.: H. J. Kramer/New World Library, 2000.

* Nelson, Mary Carroll. *Beyond Fear: The Teachings of Don Miguel Ruiz.* Tulsa, Okla.: Council Oaks Books, 1997.

* Redfield, James. *The Celestine Prophecy Series.* New York: Warner Books, Inc., 1993.

* Regardie, Israel. *The One Year Manual.* Revised edition. York Beach, Maine: Samuel Weiser, Inc., 1981.

* Ruiz, Don Miguel. *Mastery of Love.* San Rafael, Calif.: Amber-Allen Publishing, Inc., 1999.

* ———. *The Four Agreements*. San Rafael, Calif.: Amber-Allen Publishing, Inc., 1997.

* Ruiz, Don Miguel, and Janet Mills. *The Four Agreements Companion Book*. San Rafael, Calif.: Amber-Allen Publishing, Inc., 2000.

* Ruiz, Don Miguel, with Janet Mills. *The Voice of Knowledge*. San Rafael, Calif.: Amber-Allen Publishing, Inc., 2004.

Sams, Jamie. *Dancing the Dream*. New York: HarperSanFrancisco/HarperCollins, 1998.

* Small, Jacquelyn. *Embodying Spirit*. New York: HarperCollins Publishers, 1994.

* Tolle, Eckhart. *A New Earth: Awakening to Your Life's Purpose*. New York: Penguin Books, Dutton Adult, 2005.

* ———. *The Power of Now*. Novato, Calif.: New World Library, 1999.

* Vigil, Dona Bernadette. *Mastery of Awareness*. Rochester, Vt: Bear & Co., 2001.

Walsch, Neale Donald. *Conversations with God*. New York: G. P. Putnam's Sons, 1996.

* Wilber, Ken. *A Brief History of Everything*. Boston, Mass.: Shambhala, 1996.

Zukav, Gary. *The Seat of the Soul*. New York: Fireside/Simon & Schuster, 1990.

Yoga

Christensen, Alice. *The American Yoga Association Beginner's Manual*. New York: Fireside/Simon & Schuster, 1987.

* Iyengar, B. K. S. *Yoga: The Path to Holistic Health*. New York: DK Publishing, DK Adult, 2001.

* Lasiter, Judith. *Living Your Yoga.* Berkeley, Calif.: Rodmell Press, 1999.

* Yee, Rodney. *Yoga: The Poetry of the Body.* New York: St. Martin's Press, 2002.

* Yoga Journal's Series of Yoga VHS Tapes & DVDs. Healing Arts Publishing, Inc. (www.livingarts.com).

Reiki

* Stein, Diane. *Essential Reiki.* Fourth printing. Freedom, Calif.: The Crossing Press, Inc., 1996.

Natural Healing

Achterberg, Jeanne. *Imagery in Healing.* Boston, Mass.: Shambhala, 1985.

* Balch, James, and Phyllis Balch. *Prescription for Natural Healing.* New York: Avery Publishing Group, 1997.

Borysenko, Joan. *Minding the Body, Mending the Mind.* Reading, Mass.: Addison Wesley, 1987; New York: Bantam Books, 1988.

Campbell, Joseph, with Bill Moyers. *The Power of Myth.* New York: Doubleday, 1988.

Cameron, Myra. *Lifetime Encyclopedia of Natural Remedies.* New York: Parker Publishing Co., 1993.

* Chopra, Deepak. *Ageless Body, Timeless Mind: The Quantum Alternative to Growing Old.* New York: Harmony Books, 1993.

———. *Quantum Healing: Exploring the Frontiers of Mind/Body Medicine.* Reprint edition. New York: Bantam Books, 1990.

Faelten, Sharon. *The Allergy Self-Help Book.* Emmans, Pa.: Rodale Books, 1983.

Heinerman, John. *Heinerman's Encyclopedia of Fruits, Vegetables, and Herbs.* New York: Parker Publishing Co., 1998.

Lad, Vasant. *Ayurveda: The Science of Self-Healing.* Twin Lakes, Wis.: Lotus Press, 1990.

————. *Ayurveda: The Science of Life.* Audio tapes. Boulder, Colo.: Sounds True, 1994.

Payne, Mark. *Super Health in a Toxic World.* Hammersmith, London: Thorsons/HarperCollins Publishers, 1992.

Sachs, Judith. *Nature's Guide to Emotional Health and Healing.* Englewood Cliffs, N.J.: Prentice Hall, 1997.

Siegel, Bernie S. *Love, Medicine & Miracles.* New York: Harper & Row Publishers, 1986.

————. *Peace, Love & Healing.* New York: Harper & Row Publishers, 1989.

Simon, David, and Deepak Chopra. *The Chopra Center Herbal Handbook.* New York: Three Rivers Press, 2000.

Tiwari, Maya. *Ayurveda: A Life of Balance.* Rochester, Vt.: Healing Arts Press, 1995.

Weber, Tammy and Mildred Carter. *Body Reflexology.* Revised and updated version. West Nyack, N.Y.: Parker Publishing Co., 1994.

* Weil, Andrew. *8 Weeks to Optimum Health.* New York: Alfred A. Knopf, 1997.

* ————. *Spontaneous Healing: How to Discover and Embrace Your Body's Natural Ability to Maintain and Heal Itself.* New York: Ballantine Books, 2000.

Visualization

Denning, Melita, and Osborne Phillips. *The Llewellyn Practical Guide to Creative Visualization.* Second edition. St. Paul, Minn.: Llewellyn Publications, 1985.

* Gawain, Shakti. *Creative Visualization.* Twenty-fifth anniversary edition. New York: New World Library, 2002.

Miller, Emmett. *Self Imagery: Creating Your Own Good Health.* Berkeley, Calif.: Celestial Arts, 1986.

Naparstek, Belleruth. *Staying Well with Guided Imagery.* New York: Warner Books, Inc., 1994.

Meditation

Chodron, Pema. *Good Medicine.* Audio tapes. Boulder, Colo.: Sounds True, 1999.

———. *The Wisdom of No Escape.* Boston: Shambhala Publications, 1991.

Davis, Roy Eugene. *An Easy Guide to Meditation.* Revised and enlarged edition. Bethesda, Md.: CSA Press, 1988.

* Nhat Hanh, Thich. *Taming the Tiger Within: Meditations on Transforming Difficult Emotions.* New York: Penguin Group, 2004; New York: Riverhead Books, 2004.

* ———. *The Miracle of Mindfulness: A Manual on Meditation.* Revised edition. Boston, Mass.: Beacon Press, 1987.

Suzuki, Shunryu. *Zen Mind, Beginner's Mind.* Twelfth paperback printing. New York & Tokyo: John Weatherhill, Inc., 1979.

Shamanism

Arrien, Angeles. *Gathering Medicine*. Audio tapes. Boulder, Colo.: Sounds True, 1994.

* Brown, Tom, Jr. *Awakening Spirits*. New York: Berkley Books, 1994.

* Cowan, Eliot. *Plant Spirit Medicine*. Columbus, N.C.: Swan Raven & Co., 1991.

Cowan, Tom. *Fire in the Head: Shamanism and the Celtic Spirit*. New York: HarperSanFrancisco / HarperCollins, 1993.

* ———. *Shamanism: A Spiritual Practice for Daily Life*. Freedom, Calif.: The Crossing Press, 1996.

Eliade, Mircea. *Shamanism: Archaic Techniques of Ecstasy*. Second printing. Princeton, N.J.: Princeton University Press, 1974.

* Harner, Michael. *The Way of the Shaman*. Third edition. New York: HarperSanFrancisco / HarperCollins, 1990.

* Ingerman, Sandra. *A Fall to Grace*. Santa Fe, N.M.: Moon Tree Rising Productions, 1997.

* ———. *Shamanic Journeying: A Beginner's Guide*. Boulder, Colo.: Sounds True, 2004.

* ———. *Soul Retrieval, Mending the Fragmented Self*. New York: HarperSanFrancisco / HarperCollins, 1991.

* ———. *Welcome Home: Following Your Soul's Journey Home*. New York: HarperSanFrancisco / HarperCollins, 1993.

Lee, Patrick Jasper. *We Borrow the Earth: An Intimate Portrait of the Gypsy Shamanic Tradition and Culture*. U.K.: Thorsons Publishers, 2000.

* McGaa, Ed, Eagle Man. *Mother Earth Spirituality*. New York: HarperSanFrancisco / HarperCollins, 1990.

Noble, Vicki. *Shakti Woman*. New York: HarperSanFrancisco/ HarperCollins, 1991.

Prechtel, Martin. *Secrets of the Talking Jaguar.* New York: Jeremy Tarcher/Putnam, 1998.

Rain, Mary Summer. *Earthway.* New York: Pocket Books/Simon & Schuster, 1990.

* Stevens, Jose and Lena Stevens. *Secrets of Shamanism.* New York: The Philip Lief Group, Avon Books, 1988.

Wesselman, Hank. *Medicinemaker: Mystic Encounters on the Shaman's Path.* Reprint edition. New York: Bantam Books, 1999.

————. *Spiritwalker: Messages from the Future.* Reprint edition. New York: Bantam Books, 1996.

Whitely, Richard. *The Corporate Shaman.* New York: Harper-Collins Publishers, 2002.

Totems

* Andrews, Ted. *Animal Speak.* St. Paul, Minn.: Llewellyn Publications, 1997.

* ————. *Animal Wise.* Jackson, Tenn.: Dragonhawk Publishing, 1999.

* ————. *Animal Wise Tarot Cards.* Jackson, Tenn.: Dragonhawk Publishing, 1999.

* ————. *Nature-Speak.* Jackson, Tenn.: Dragonhawk Publishing, 2004.

Conway, D. J. *Animal Magick.* St. Paul, Minn.: Llewellyn Publications, 1996; New York: DK Adult, 2001.

Sams, Jamie. *Animal Medicine.* Audio tapes. Boulder, Colo.: Sounds True, 1997.

* Sams, Jamie, and Avid Carson. *Medicine Cards.* Revised, expanded edition. New York: St. Martin's Press, 1999.

Healing Music

Coyote OldMan: Allen, Michael Graham, and Michael Fitzsimmons. *In Medicine River.* Berryville, Ark.: Coyote OldMan Music, 1992.

Das, Krishna. *All One.* New York: Karuna Music/Triloka Records, 2005.

———. *Live on Earth.* New York: Karuna LLC, 2002.

Fitzgerald, Scott. *Thunderdrums.* Friday Harbor, San Juan Island, Wash.: World Disc Productions, Inc., 1990. 1-800-228-5711.

Goldman, Jonathon. Ultimate OM. Etherean Music. 1-888-384-3732. www.ethereanmusic.com.

Gordon, Steve and David. *Sacred Earth Drums.* Sequoia Records, 1994. 1-800-524-5513.

———. *Sacred Spirit Drums.* Sequoia Records, 1996. 1-800-524-5513.

Halpern, Steven. *Higher Ground, Alpha & Theta Brainwave Music.* San Anselmo, Calif.: Open Channel Sound. 1-800-726-3924 (ext. 7848).

Holly, Tery. *Atlantis.* So Su Me Music. http://hometown.aol.com/beechlady/Spot/index.html.

———. *Celtic Om.* So Su Me Music. http://hometown.aol.com/beechlady/Spot/index.html.

———. *Far Vista.* So Su Me Music. http://hometown.aol.com/beechlady/Spot/index.html.

———. *Great Waters.* So Su Me Music. http://hometown.aol.com/beechlady/Spot/index.html.

————. *Thesmophoria*. So Su Me Music. http://hometown.aol.com/beechlady/Spot/index.html.

————. *Whatever*. So Su Me Music. http://hometown.aol.com/beechlady/Spot/index.html.

Jamieson, Sita. *Presence: Chants of Sacred Power*. Sita Jamieson, 2003.

Mirabal, Robert. *Land*. Burbank, Calif.: Warner Bros. Records, Inc., 1995. www.mirabal.com.

————. *Mirabal: Alter-Native*. Burbank, Calif.: Warner Bros. Records, Inc. 1997. www.mirabal.com.

————. *Music from a Painted Cave*. Boulder, Colo.: Silver Wave Records, Inc. 2001. www.mirabal.com.

————. *Song Carrier*. Boulder, Colo.: Silver Wave Records, Inc. 1995. www.mirabal.com.

Mock, Andreas. *Merlin's Magic: Light Reiki Touch*. Boulder, Colo.: Inner Worlds Music, 1995. 1-800-444-9678.

————. *Merlin's Magic: The Heart of Reiki*. Boulder, Colo.: Inner Worlds Music, 1997. 1-800-444-9678.

Nakai, R. Carlos. *Emergence, Songs of the Rainbow World*. Phoenix, Ariz.: Canyon Records Productions, 1992.

Natural Wonders, a compilation from. *Virtual Journey*. 1-800-771-0987.

North Word Press, Inc. *Nature Quest: An Adventure in Nature and Music: Woodland Voices*. U.K.: Gallant.

Raye, Marina. *Blissful Journey: Music to Nurture the Soul*. Penrose, Calif.: Native Heart Music, 2001. www.marinaraye.com.

————. *Nature's Enchantment*. Penrose, Calif.: Native Heart Music, 2004. www.marinaraye.com.